REGENTS RENAISSANCE DRAMA SERIES

General Editor: Cyrus Hoy
Advisory Editor: G. E. Bentley

THE MALCONTENT

JOHN MARSTON

The Malcontent

Edited by

M. L. WINE

UNIVERSITY OF NEBRASKA PRESS · LINCOLN

Library of Congress Catalog Card Number: 64–17228

MANUFACTURED IN THE UNITED STATES OF AMERICA

Regents Renaissance Drama Series

The purpose of the Regents Renaissance Drama Series is to provide soundly edited texts, in modern spelling, of the more significant plays of the Elizabethan, Jacobean, and Caroline theater. Each text in the series is based on a fresh collation of all sixteenth- and seventeenth-century editions. The textual notes, which appear above the line at the bottom of each page, record all substantive departures from the edition used as the copy-text. Variant substantive readings among sixteenth- and seventeenth-century editions are listed there as well. In cases where two or more of the old editions present widely divergent readings, a list of substantive variants in editions through the seventeenth century is given in an appendix. Editions after 1700 are referred to in the textual notes only when an emendation originating in some one of them is received into the text. Variants of accidentals (spelling, punctuation, capitalization) are not recorded in the notes. Contracted forms of characters' names are silently expanded in speech prefixes and stage directions, and, in the case of speech prefixes, are regularized. Additions to the stage directions of the copy-text are enclosed in brackets. Stage directions such as "within" or "aside" are enclosed in parentheses when they occur in the copy-text.

Spelling has been modernized along consciously conservative lines. "Murther" has become "murder," and "burthen," "burden," but within the limits of a modernized text, and with the following exceptions, the linguistic quality of the original has been carefully preserved. The variety of contracted forms (*'em*, *'am*, *'m*, *'um*, *'hem*) used in the drama of the period for the pronoun *them* are here regularly given as *'em*, and the alternation between *a'th'* and *o'th'* (for *on* or *of the*) is regularly reproduced as *o'th'*. The copy-text distinction between preterite endings in *-d* and *-ed* is preserved except where the elision of *e* occurs in the penultimate syllable; in such cases, the final syllable is contracted. Thus, where the old editions read "threat'ned," those of the present series read "threaten'd." Where, in the old editions, a contracted preterite in *-y'd* would yield *-i'd* in modern spelling (as in "try'd," "cry'd," "deny'd"), the word is here given in its full form (e.g., "tried," "cried," "denied").

Punctuation has been brought into accord with modern practices. The effort here has been to achieve a balance between the generally light pointing of the old editions, and a system of punctuation which, without overloading the text with exclamation marks, semicolons, and dashes, will make the often loosely flowing verse (and prose) of the original syntactically intelligible to the modern reader. Dashes are regularly used only to indicate interrupted speeches, or shifts of address within a single speech.

Explanatory notes, chiefly concerned with glossing obsolete words and phrases, are printed below the textual notes at the bottom of each page. References to stage directions in the notes follow the admirable system of the Revels editions, whereby stage directions are keyed, decimally, to the line of the text before or after which they occur. Thus, a note on 0.2 has reference to the second line of the stage direction at the beginning of the scene in question. A note on 115.1 has reference to the first line of the stage direction following line 115 of the text of the relevant scene.

CYRUS HOY

University of Rochester

Contents

Acknowledgments

For the present edition of *The Malcontent* I have collated directly the thirty-six extant quartos of the three 1604 editions, but even more than my textual and explanatory notes would indicate I owe much to all modern editors from Dodsley on.

A grant from the Research and Publications Committee of Claremont Graduate School enabled me to procure microfilms of all the quartos and to prepare the edition for publication. I am grateful to the Committee and to its chairman, Dr. David W. Davies, as well as to the libraries and institutions cited in the Introduction that so generously granted microfilming permission.

Professor Sears Jayne made many helpful suggestions, and Professor Allan Casson not only helped with the arduous task of proofreading but also assisted in a number of other ways. The general editor has been unfailingly generous with his time and assistance. To each of them I wish to express my thanks.

M. L. W.

List of Abbreviations

B-H-N	C. R. Baskervill, V. B. Heltzel, and A. H. Nethercot, eds. *Elizabethan and Stuart Plays*. New York, 1934.
B-P	C. F. T. Brooke and N. B. Paradise, eds. *English Drama 1580–1642*. Boston, 1933.
Bullen	A. H. Bullen, ed. *The Works of John Marston*. Vol. I. London, 1887.
Dodsley	Robert Dodsley. *A Select Collection of Old Plays*.
Collier Gilchrist Reed Steevens	Ed. J. P. Collier, 3rd ed. Vol. IV. London, 1825–1827.* (with annotations by Isaac Reed, Octavius Gilchrist, George Steevens, and John Payne Collier.)
Dyce	Rev. A. Dyce, ed. *The Works of John Webster*. London, 1871.*
Halliwell	J. O. Halliwell[-Phillipps], ed. *The Works of John Marston*. Vol. II. London, 1856.
Harrison	G. B. Harrison, ed. *The Malcontent*. London, 1933.
Lucas	F. L. Lucas, ed. The Induction to *The Malcontent* in *The Complete Works of John Webster*. Vol. III. London, 1927.
MP	*Modern Philology*
Neilson	W. A. Neilson, ed. *The Chief Elizabethan Dramatists*. Boston, 1911.
OED	*Oxford English Dictionary*
PBSA	*Papers of the Bibliographical Society of America*
PQ	*Philological Quarterly*
Q	Copy-text: Third Quarto of 1604
Q1	First Quarto of 1604
Q2	Second Quarto of 1604
Qq	All three quartos of 1604

* Earlier editions of Dodsley (1744, 1780) and of Dyce (1830, 1857) have been consulted, but the final editions in which *The Malcontent* appears reprint virtually the same texts and add to the explanatory notes. Sir Walter Scott's *The Ancient British Drama* (London, 1810, Vol. II) merely reprints the text of Dodsley's 1780 edition and adds nothing in the way of annotation.

List of Abbreviations

RES	*Review of English Studies*
S.D.	Stage direction
S.P.	Speech prefix
SP	*Studies in Philology*
Spencer	H. Spencer, ed. *Elizabethan Plays*. Boston, 1933.
Wood	H. H. Wood, ed. *The Plays of John Marston*. Vol. I. Edinburgh, 1934.

Introduction

TEXT

"An Enterlude called *the Malecontent*[,] *Tragiecomedia*," was entered in the Stationers' Register, in the names of William Aspley and Thomas Thorpe, on July 5, 1604, and was published in that same year, presumably, in three quarto editions. The date "1604" appears in an unusual position on the title pages of all three editions: just below the center ornament and not with the imprint at the bottom of the page. Thus, as Sir Walter Greg has pointed out, "the position of the date on the title is such that it need not necessarily refer to the printing: at the same time there appears no reason to doubt that all three did appear in the second half of 1604."[1] The chronology of the three editions is not difficult to determine: the second corrects errors in the first and adds new material; the third corrects errors in the second, includes the new material, and contains considerable additions found in neither of the other two quartos.[2]

The title page of the first edition reads as follows:

> *THE*/ MALCONTENT./ By John Marston./ [ornament]/ 1604./ Printed at London by V. S. for *William Aspley*,/ and are to be solde at his shop in Paules/ Church-yard.

The printer, for this and the other two quartos, was undoubtedly Valentine Simmes. Extant copies of the first edition contain corrected and uncorrected states in several formes (inner B, outer E, and inner G), but the edition in general gives the impression that it was carelessly set from a manuscript that was probably difficult to follow. Marston's own policy, as he tells us in the prefatory remarks to this play and to others, was to see that the printer received an authoritative copy, but thereafter he relied "much . . . upon the printer's

[1] W. W. Greg, *A Bibliography of the English Printed Drama to the Restoration* (London, 1939), I, 322, where complete details of the collation of all three editions are given.

[2] W. W. Greg, "Notes on Old Books," *The Library*, II (1921), 51.

discretion." The printer's discretion in this case was not very good.[3]

The title page of the second edition is almost the same as that of the first, except that the imprint has been reset and the order of words slightly changed.[4] Changes in the text, such as that at I.ii.14 (from "I'll pray" to "I'll go to church"), would seem to indicate that Marston himself submitted to the printer a roughly corrected copy. A prologue and an epilogue have been added. Much of the type of the first edition was kept standing for the second, although many pages reveal minor corrections, the resetting of type that had fallen to pieces when the formes were unlocked, and the resetting of whole passages.[5] Among the extant copies, corrected and uncorrected states exist in several formes, most notably in inner and outer B and in inner and outer G. The copy in the Carl H. Pforzheimer Library, which apparently Greg did not examine, contains one whole sheet (G) which has been completely recast, differing from all other copies of this edition. Copies of the second edition are very rare, and apparently the printer stopped the presses very early because of more corrections and additions coming in; very likely the Pforzheimer copy represents a transitional stage, for a number of readings in its recast sheet influenced the third edition.

The title page of the third edition is identical to that of the second except for the change in the authorship ascription:

> Augmented by *Marston.*/ With the *A*dditions played by the Kings Maiesties servants./ Written by *Ihon Webster*.

The "augmentations" consist of many new passages in the text and, of course, the Induction. The text is entirely recast and, on the whole, follows the corrections made in the second edition although some stage directions have dropped out. Copies of this edition are considerably more numerous than those of the other editions, but no more than one impression seems to have been made.

[3] A copy of this edition was included in a nonce collection of Marston's *Comedies, Tragicomedies, and Tragedies* in 1652.

[4] "AT LONDON/ Printed by V. S. for William Aspley, and/ are to be sold at his shop in Paules/ Church-yard."

[5] Greg, "Notes on Old Books," pp. 51–52. R. E. Brettle, "More Bibliographical Notes on Marston," *The Library*, XII (1931), 240–241, observes that the inner and outer formes of sheet E, inner D, and inner and outer A are practically untouched. See also Fredson Bowers, "Notes on Standing Type in Elizabethan Printing," *PBSA*, XL (1946), 205–224.

The third, the "augmented," edition must be, of course, the copy-text for any subsequent edition. The seeming contradiction between its title page and the head-title to the Induction ("THE/ INDVCTION TO/ THE MALECONTENT, AND/ the additions acted by the Kings Ma-/ iesties servants./ Written by *John Webster*.") has led to some debate over the extent to which the additions can be ascribed to Marston; but most scholars agree now that the play itself was "augmented by *Marston*," as the title page indicates, and that Webster wrote the Induction, that is, "the Additions played by the Kings Maiesties servants."[6] If Webster did collaborate on the additions, it is a thankless task to try to distinguish his fragments from Marston's, since Marston seems to have influenced the style of the early Webster.

Although it contains many corrections and has some gatherings that exist in corrected and uncorrected states, the third edition has been poorly proofread. Like the earlier quartos, it has its source in an authorial copy that possibly had been worked over in the theater;[7] and the present edition does not scruple to incorporate into the copy-text readings from the earlier quartos if they are justifiable. Where the copy-text differs from these, and it is not clear whether a genuine correction was intended, the reading of the copy-text remains if it is a good one; thus at I.ii.9 *ragged* is retained even though the first two quartos read *rugged*. On the other hand, where evidence exists of carelessness on the part of the compositor, readings from the earlier quartos are preferred; thus at I.vi.23 *jaw'd* (*iawde* in the first two quartos) replaces *jade* (*iade* in the copy-text) because it seems clear that the compositor carelessly dropped the *w* (*jaw'd* makes better sense and is a word that Marston uses several times in combination, as at I.vii.1 and at IV.iii.97).[8] At III.ii.49 the compositor apparently was thinking ahead and simply ran together *Ithaca, can* (first two quartos) into *Ithacan*; and at II.iv.2, working in a more compressed text, he reduced *methodically* to *methodical* to justify the line where earlier compositors felt no need to save space. The textual notes record all divergences from the copy-text, as well as interesting variants in the earlier quartos.

[6] See, in particular, the argument of E. E. Stoll, *John Webster* (Boston, 1905), pp. 59–62.

[7] See Wilfred T. Jewkes, *Act Division in Elizabethan and Jacobean Plays, 1583–1616* (Hamden, Conn., 1958), pp. 263–264.

[8] See also V.ii.56 (*come/ cowe*), V.v.34 (*warpt/ wrapt*), V.vi.33 (*forfeited/ forteified*), V.vi.66 (*court/ count*).

For the present edition, the following copies of the three 1604 editions have been collated:

First Edition: Bodleian Library of Oxford University, British Museum, Folger Shakespeare Library (two copies), Henry E. Huntington Library (two copies), Pierpont Morgan Library, New York Public Library, Carl H. Pforzheimer Library, and Victoria and Albert Museum.

Second Edition: Boston Public Library, British Museum, Library of Congress, Henry E. Huntington Library, Carl H. Pforzheimer Library, University of Sheffield Library.

Third Edition: Bodleian Library (two copies), Boston Public Library, British Museum (three copies), Eton College Library, Folger Shakespeare Library (three copies), Houghton Library of Harvard University, Henry E. Huntington Library (two copies), University of Michigan Library, New York Public Library, Carl H. Pforzheimer Library, University of Texas Library, Yale University Library, and Victoria and Albert Museum (two copies).

DATE

Dating *The Malcontent* continues to be a vexing problem in the study of Tudor-Stuart drama, scholarly opinion veering between around 1600 and the year of publication. No one disputes 1604 as the date of the Induction, particularly since it contains an allusion (l. 33) to Osric's speech in *Hamlet* (V.ii.105) that appears only in the second quarto (1604) of that play and also a possible allusion to the needy Scottish followers of James I (l. 93 and note). However, in the Induction, Sly says, "I am one that hath seen this play often"; and the question is, how long before the King's Men appropriated the play that Marston originally wrote for a boys' company could Sly have seen it. As early as 1905–1906, E. E. Stoll argued for about 1600, making the cornerstone of his argument the pamphlet of 1588 which Octavius Gilchrist cited in the 1825 Dodsley edition of the play to explain the allusion at I.viii.18–20 to a horn "growing in the woman's forehead twelve years since."[9] Twelve years later would be,

[9] Stoll, *Webster*, pp. 55–60; also "Shakespere, Marston and the Malcontent Type," *MP*, III (1906), 281–303; and "The Date of *The Malcontent*: A Rejoinder," *RES*, XI (1935), 42–50.

of course, 1600. As it happens, this passage occurs in one of the additions to the third edition; and Stoll argued that Marston must have restored passages for the Globe performance which were cut at the Blackfriars to allow enough time for the musical interludes that were an integral part of the evening's entertainment at the private theater. Stoll also maintained that Marston's Malevole influenced Shakespeare's characterizations of Hamlet and Jaques.

The consensus of critical opinion, however, following Chambers and Walley and Lucas,[10] inclines towards the later date, arguing that the number "twelve" is to be taken as a round number only; that the reference in the first edition at V.v.23 to *S. Andrew Iaques* is a satirical allusion to James I that had to be cut from subsequent editions (although it may be an interpolation also); that Hamlet and Jaques, though malcontent figures, hardly reflect the character of Malevole and that the "comicall satyres" of Jonson were a greater influence on Marston than Marston was on Shakespeare; that the fool Passarello, an addition to the third edition, would be an important character in the adult company but not in the boys' company and, therefore, was created expressly by Marston for the King's Men; and that the allusions in the Induction to earlier performances at the Blackfriars would indicate that the play was Marston's first effort for the newly-formed Children of the Queen's Revels in which he had acquired a one-sixth interest in February, 1604 (although, of course, he could have dredged up a play written earlier, and no one can be sure what his associations were with Blackfriars before 1604). Furthermore, since the same printer printed the unaugmented and the augmented editions within a relatively short time of one another, it is not likely that the play was literally "lost," as the Induction indicates, and that Marston did not know in advance of the Globe production. Indeed, the third edition has indications of authorial revision, as, for example, at II.ii.28, where a speech given to Maquerelle in the earlier editions has been transferred to Biancha and another stage direction and line of dialogue added to make the transfer intelligible—an augmentation that would not materially have affected the abridgment of music in the public theater.

Recently, however, Gustav Cross has championed the earlier date (around 1600), maintaining that *The Malcontent* more closely

[10] E. K. Chambers, *The Elizabethan Stage* (Oxford, 1933), III, 431–432; Harold R. Walley, "The Date of *Hamlet* and Marston's *The Malcontent*," *RES*, IX (1933), 397–409; Lucas, pp. 294–295.

resembles the revenge-type plays that Marston was writing at the turn of the century; that it is closer in verbal parallels to the satires that Marston was writing in the late 1590's; that, like the satires rather than the later plays, it has a higher proportion of neologisms; and that it alludes to works written around 1600 rather than to Montaigne's *Essaies* upon which Marston so heavily leaned after Florio's translation appeared in 1603. Cross concludes his case "with what must be final and incontrovertible proof that *The Malcontent* was indeed written *c.* 1600, and that is the testimony to this effect of the dramatist himself": a passage in *The Fawn* (which Cross dates 1604) that appears to refer to the discovery by "the old Duke Pietro" of *The Malcontent* to his wife's infidelity four years earlier.[11]

Cross's arguments are plausible and carry conviction; yet, in the last analysis, they are not "final and incontrovertible." Even more recently, Anthony Caputi has suggested, to make sense of Sly's remark, that the play was probably a Blackfriars' success just before the closing of the theaters in May of 1603 because of the plague and that the King's Men negotiated to use it for the reopening of the Globe in April of 1604: "it is rather improbable that the managers at Blackfriars would have permitted Marston to transfer a play to the Globe that they had produced only recently, perhaps were still producing, and also improbable that the managers of the Globe would have wanted it."[12] Caputi's implied designation of 1602–1603 may be the most judicious.

Aside from its original performances by the boys' company at the Blackfriars and by the King's Men at the Globe, attested to in the Induction, the only other evidence of a contemporary performance of *The Malcontent* is the one that John Greene records in his diary as having seen in February, 1634/1635.[13]

THE PLAY

Though it includes near-murders, virtue in distress, moral reclamations, a Machiavellian villain, and dissolute and corrupt specimens of mankind, *The Malcontent* is actually a very funny play. Malevole's

[11] Gustav Cross, "The Date of *The Malcontent* Once More," *PQ*, XXXIX (1960), 104–113.

[12] Anthony Caputi, *John Marston, Satirist* (Ithaca, 1961), pp. 265–266.

[13] G. E. Bentley, *The Jacobean and Caroline Stage* (Oxford, 1941), I, 123. Bentley assumes that the play was performed at Blackfriars.

game of outfoxing the villains and of underlining the moral sickness and absurdity of the flunkies who adorn the court of Genoa is at once reassuring and entertaining; a number of scenes have no direct relationship to the major action and are clearly comic; and the sheer verbal fecundity of some of the most bitter and satirical passages renders even the "hideous imagination" of Malevole and other characters in the play hilarious. The common charge against Marston that he undoes the seriousness of his themes by the excesses of his satirical language, his melodramatic stage effects, and his seeming disregard for the motivation of his characters completely misses the point. The frank confession of theatricalism is at the heart of the play's meaning. Marston was fond of asserting that he strove to delight rather than to instruct; but the choice of his particular comic form was for him clearly ethical, as well as esthetic. In the prefatory "To the Reader" he insists upon the fiction of his play—the setting, the characters—and defends the *freedom* the satiric form entitles him to, just as Burbage, in the Induction, defends "the ancient freedom of poesy." Marston would undoubtedly agree with those playwrights today who find in humor a source of creative liberty, for it is, in M. Ionesco's words, "the intuition of the absurd": by dislocating the obvious, it is a means of disengaging us from ordinary perceptions and of forcing us to evaluate experience afresh. The evident theatrical humor of plays like *The Malcontent* turns plot into a dramatic metaphor of absurdity.

The Malcontent deals, of course, with many serious themes: social, political, and moral corruption; the gullibility and the ineffectiveness of the merely good in a fallen world. Indeed, the Christian overtones that pervade the play relate it in many ways to the medieval morality play. The Duchess Maria at one point says, "Here round about is hell"; and the Genoese court does suggest a godless universe, which is ultimately defeated only by the grace of Providence, to which even Malevole attributes his success:

> Who doubts of Providence,
> That sees this change? (IV.v.136–137)

But though these themes are serious, the play does not give an immediate impression of taking itself too seriously. The opening scene in which the two courtiers rant about Malevole's "vilest out-of-tune music" and the subsequent scene that prepares for the introduction of Malevole prevent a serious mood from developing. And when he does enter finally, Malevole seems so to fit Pietro's description of him that he is at first difficult to take seriously:

> This Malevole is one of the most prodigious affections that ever convers'd with nature: a man, or rather a monster, more discontent than Lucifer when he was thrust out of the presence. . . . See, he comes. Now shall you hear the extremity of a malcontent. (I.ii.16–19—I.iii.1–2)

Then, as the intrigue and counter-intrigue develop, and as we come to understand Malevole's role better, we cannot help but be assured that all will turn out well. By the end of the second act, Malevole is in full control of the situation:

> The beauty of the day begins to rise,
> From whose bright form night's heavy shadow flies.
> Now 'gins close plots to work; the scene grows full,
> And craves his eyes who hath a solid skull.
>
> (II.v.156–159)

Halfway through the play, in the middle of the third act, "the wind begins to come about," and the happy end is in sight. Mendoza proves to be such an extreme villain, so serenely confident in himself as a "wise man," that he becomes an easy puppet for Malevole, whom he even employs, to manipulate.

Melodramatic and absurd? Yes, of course; but as an intuition of the absurd, *The Malcontent* is not an ordinary Tudor-Stuart revenge play or play of intrigue: the intrigue and counter-intrigue are themselves metaphors of absurdity. Evil and corruption may not be something to laugh at, but from a broad social and moral outlook—an outlook that recognizes the inherent difficulty of the human situation and endeavors to give it some value—the picture of humanity creating a web of trickery and deception and then getting enmeshed in it is ultimately ludicrous. The broad perspective reaffirms the comic and humane virtues of freedom, love, order, and harmony; the narrow perspective adumbrates only servility, lust, disorder, and chaos. And it is from the heavy shadows of this narrow and uncongenial world that the enlightened hero of comedy attempts to bring forth light from the void. Hence the melodrama of the play and the ultimate triumph of the good: the tragic quest for enlightenment and self-mastery is not the question here, but rather the comic goal of a society restored to sanity.

The Malcontent, then, is a study in deception, and the mask-disguise is the central dramatic symbol; when the *masquers* step forth at the end of the play and reveal themselves, they herald the triumph of the humane world and the restoration of order. The convention of the masque becomes in the play a dramatic pun, and until that moment the *brawl* danced in the fourth act is symbolic—just as Malevole's vile, discordant music is—of the absurd world of the play. By contrast, and signaling the world to come, the "sirenical" melodies sung by the pages are, in their concord, out of tune with the court of Genoa.[14] Where deception rules, intrigue is the way of the world; and imagery of the hunt or the chase reflects this topsy-turvy world of humanity copreying upon itself. Mendoza gloats over the scheme he has concocted to catch his rival in lust, Ferneze: "He's caught; the woodcock's head is i' th' noose." Bilioso uses his wife and daughter-in-law as bait to promote his own advancement in court. Malevole calls Maquerelle "the duke's lime-twig"—the trap for ensnaring birds, or, in the context of the play, innocent maidens. Maria refuses to "stoop to the duke's [Mendoza's] lure." And Pietro, already on the road to enlightenment and repentance, refrains from joining the chase: "As for me, 'tis unfit one beast should hunt another."

A courtly facade of manners covers deception almost everywhere. Aurelia is faithless to her husband and even to her lover. Mendoza, besides cuckolding his best friend, writes "passionate flashes" (sonnets), like Castiglione's noble courtier, to his ideal lady, whom he loves only because she is a duchess who can lead him to material preferment rather than up the scale of love to a vision of the True and the Good; later, he confesses to Malevole that he loves Maria with "no great affection, but as wise men do love great women, to ennoble their blood and augment their revenue." The courtier Bilioso, a "dear Castilio" (that is, Castiglione) himself, is a pimp to his wife and to his daughter-in-law, and "had rather stand with wrong than fall with right." The court bawd—an almost official position—instructs the ladies in the art of appearing virtuous and of hiding their years: the whole of Act II, scene iv, where Maquerelle gives detailed instructions in the art of preparing restorative possets,

[14] See Christian Kiefer, "Music and Marston's *The Malcontent*," *SP*, LI (1954), 163–171.

is a study in deception itself. Even the fool Passarello recognizes that his mask brings him food and clothing at least; and the one truly virtuous person, Celso, is forced to talk in asides.

The court betrays the ideals of the courtier and of the humanist conception of man: as Malevole observes, wise men and philosophical monarchs are no more than natural fools, and the courtier who happens to be a scholar by art is no more than a fool by nature.[15] Even Pietro has a dig at the Stoic "wise man": "Out upon [Seneca]! He writ of temperance and fortitude, yet lived like a voluptuous epicure and died like an effeminate coward." In Marston's fictitious Genoa the Elizabethan ideal of the court—society at its highest point of refinement—is viewed through disenchanted eyes: we are clearly on the threshold of Jacobean drama. The gulf between what men profess to be and what they are looms large now, so that, as the Prologue warns, who writes of men must write of fools.

The double figure of Altofronto-Malevole is one of Marston's most inspired creations. Traditionally, the satirist is a passive figure who rails at the human comedy as a spectator rather than as a participant. But by actively involving his satirist-railer in the plot of his "comicall satyre," Marston gives greater urgency to his railings and at the same time creates a figure who, straddling the two worlds of the play, gives us the assurance of the broad perspective. As Altofronto, the protagonist assures us that the humane world will triumph, at least in the play. Malevole is not one side of Altofronto's character even though the career of the banished former duke of Genoa is enough to make him "the extremity of a malcontent." Malevole is a mask for survival for Altofronto, a mask that is necessary in a society where everyone dons one. As the good but ineffectual duke, wanting "those old instruments of state,/ Dissemblance and suspect," Altofronto is the victim of deception and intrigue and must succumb to them. The price of his banishment from a fool's paradise, however, is the newly earned knowledge of how to survive in a fallen world. The old duke could not have uttered the axioms of statecraft that fall so readily from Malevole's lips; but now, like Shakespeare's Duke Vincentio, he realizes the sad but awful necessity of applying "craft against vice" as a measure of self-defense. As a malcontent,

[15] Hiram Haydn, in *The Counter-Renaissance* (New York, 1950), discusses the turn-of-the-century "protest against the basic principles of the classical renaissance"; see especially his remarks on Marston in Chapter 9 ("The Courtly Traditions of Love and Honor").

a mask that his society conventionally recognizes but, ironically, does not take seriously, Malevole finds a place in court:[16]

> Well, this disguise doth yet afford me that
> Which kings do seldom hear, or great men use—
> Free speech; and though my state's usurp'd,
> Yet this affected strain gives me a tongue
> As fetterless as is an emperor's.
> I may speak foolishly, ay, knavishly,
> Always carelessly, yet no one thinks it fashion
> To poise my breath; for he that laughs and strikes
> Is lightly felt, or seldom struck again.
>
> (I.iii.158–166)

His disguise thus makes him "as free as air" to blow over every man; it enables him to vent the anger in his heart while it leaves him free to work his own counterplots against the villainy that has driven him to this recourse. And it permits him to adopt the methods of absurdity: "Illo, ho, ho, ho!" he cries out to Mendoza, luring his victim with the cry of a falconer luring his falcon.

Were it not that the mask of Malevole is necessary, Altofronto would doff it at once. The scenes in which he can relax for a moment to confide in his one trustworthy friend, Celso, are scenes of relief within the play itself: the tone becomes quiet, the shrillness of the language subsides, and for an instance we penetrate beyond the absurdity of the plot; in fact, in these scenes he reveals his schemes for creating the plot. Even then, however, he must be on guard; one of the most revealing stage directions in the entire play—revealing because it tells us so much about the acting of the play and about Malevole's awareness that he is a mask—interrupts such a scene:

> Bilioso *entering*, Malevole *shifteth his speech*.[17] (I.iv.43.1)

Sometimes even the irony that the mask allows him to evoke is too much for him, and he breaks down, as when, still disguised, he has

16 In Marston's *Antonio's Revenge*, Alberto advises the banished Antonio to return disguised as "a spitting critic, whose mouth/ Voids nothing but gentile and unvulgar/ Rheum of censure."

17 The shift is from verse to prose. In *The Question of Hamlet* (New York, 1959, pp. 117–118), Harry Levin argues that "the implicit distinction between the exterior and inward man" is indicated in *Hamlet* and in *The Malcontent* by prose (the antic disposition = the mask) and by verse (the reality).

to bear witness to his wife's exemplary steadfastness in the midst of adversity:

> Maquerelle, I tell thee, I have found an honest woman. . . . For as nowadays no courtier but has his mistress, no captain but has his cockatrice, no cuckold but has his horns, and no fool but has his feather, even so, no woman but has her weakness and feather too, no sex but has his—I can hunt the letter no farther. [*Aside.*] O God, how loathsome this toying is to me! That a duke should be forc'd to fool it!
>
> (V.iii.33–42)

But, as he hastens to observe, "Better play the fool lord than be the fool lord." The rhetoric (for that is mainly what it is) of the satire, the foolishness of his role, are more than he can bear; and the mask becomes intolerable.

The mask of Malevole, then, is a strategy for survival; and the ridiculous, conventional plot is symbolic of what a good man must struggle against. But absurdity does not demand vengeance: civilization asks for enlightenment and ultimately offers pardon. Like Hercules in Marston's *The Fawn,* Malevole is not out to get an eye for an eye, but rather to make use of human weakness to reclaim humanity from absurdity. "Discord to malcontents is very manna," he tells Celso; but his role is to bring concord out of the discord. As a servant of the Providence he invokes, he rightly considers himself a surgeon who "tents" his patients "to the ground," that is, who probes their wounds until they burst and begin to heal. Those who are not beyond salvation—Pietro, Aurelia, Ferneze—he leads to moral reawakening by shattering their benighted complacency as a first step toward their achieving the calm heart that comes from a broader vision than they have known:

> Lean thoughtfulness, a sallow meditation,
> Suck thy veins dry! Distemperance rob thy sleep!
> The heart's disquiet is revenge most deep:
> He that gets blood, the life of flesh but spills,
> But he that breaks heart's peace, the dear soul kills.
>
> (I.iii.153–157)

> Duke, I'll torment thee: now my just revenge
> From thee than crown a richer gem shall part.
> Beneath God naught's so dear as a calm heart.
>
> (I.iii.167–169)

Malevole's pessimistic and Hamlet-like speech, beginning at IV.v.107 ("Think this: this earth is the only grave and Golgotha wherein all things that live must rot"), is not meant to be taken literally. Malevole exaggerates, as his malcontent role allows him to, the pessimism when Pietro's despair is deepest; and the effect is successful, for Pietro, whose own victimization has led him to Altofronto's vision, confesses his contrition and craves "all love and pardon." Similarly, Aurelia and Ferneze are driven to repentance: they acknowledge their depravity and are forgiven. By the end, all the fools and knaves have been driven to crave pardon; and if they actually seem beyond reclamation, Mendoza and the others at least now recognize their inherently servile natures.

If the ending seems too provisional (the Mendozas and Biliosos and Maquerelles and Bianchas have changed only their places of residence; they may return), it is to remind us that comedy offers no solutions for or escapes from the human condition. "Virtue is triumphant only in theatricals," the Mikado once observed; and Malevole's final words remind us that we are in the theater:

> The rest of idle actors idly part;
> And as for me, I here assume my right,
> To which I hope all's pleas'd. To all, good night.

And if that is not enough, the Epilogus steps forth to apologize for the entire proceedings. The comedy of *The Malcontent* has served *literally to show* us not simply what fools these mortals be but how continuous is the struggle against absurdity.

When in his prefatory address to the reader he admits that he is afflicted "to think that scenes invented merely [i.e., only] to be spoken should be enforcively published to be read," Marston is not coyly trying to allay criticism of his play. In a note to a later comedy, *The Fawn*, he similarly defends himself: "Comedies are writ to be spoken, not read; remember the life of these things consists in action." All of us know, of course, that when we pick up a play to read we read only its text; the play is its entire production. In a comedy which emphasizes, as we have repeatedly emphasized, the absurdity of humans even in their capacity for evil, emphatic gesture is especially important. Moreover, in fairness to Marston, who everywhere in *The Malcontent* shows the skill of a playwright who knows the theater that he is writing for, let us recall the circumstances in which he wrote it. The boys at the private theater at Blackfriars—whether the Children of the Chapel Royal before 1604 or the Children of the Queen's Revels after—were primarily choristers, and the plays were staged in a concert atmosphere so that the evidence of theatricality was always apparent: before the play began the audience was treated to approximately an hour's interlude of music, and music filled the intervals between acts. The opening stage direction of Act II indicates how the entr'acte musical interlude frequently merged with the beginning of the ensuing act. The boys, probably no older than fourteen or fifteen (the page at the beginning of Act IV tells Maquerelle that he thinks he is fourteen, thus ironically reminding the audience how young all the actors are) and many considerably younger, were not truly serious actors. Indeed, their appeal as actors seems to have derived from their lack of utter seriousness and from their agile ability, by grace of their stature, to "ape" adult actors. It is no mere coincidence that most of the plays written for the boys' companies turn out to be satirical comedies. R. A. Foakes has pointed out recently that Marston's early two *Antonio* plays, regarded as somewhat bewilderingly "fantastical" by modern readers, were conceived as "fantastical" burlesques of contemporary adult drama and of the adult actors.[18] In conceiving *The Malcontent*, Marston most certainly must have had his actors in mind: children imitating adults reduce the adult world to childishness, and their effect is to add another dimension of absurdity—the most obvious to an audience. Furthermore, the contrast between the hour's concert and the "vilest out-of-tune music" that opens the play would be startling. The playwright could count on the effect of the music enveloping the original performances to heighten the distance, just as the child actors did, between spectator and play, and probably also to suggest a world of loveliness just briefly glimpsed at and struggled for in the play itself.

Thus Sinklo's wager in Webster's Induction—"I durst lay four of mine ears the play is not so well acted as it hath been"—may not be so foolish as it seems or even a gibe by a King's Men playwright at the boy actors for whom Marston originally wrote the play.

[18] R. A. Foakes, "John Marston's Fantastical Plays: *Antonio and Mellida* and *Antonio's Revenge*," *PQ*, XLI (1962), 229–239. For excellent discussions of the child actors, see Caputi, pp. 98–110, and H. N. Hillebrand, *The Child Actors* (Urbana, 1926), Part II, pp. 253–273.

If we may change just slightly a line addressed directly to the audience by a character in Genet's play of 1958, *The Blacks* (also a play about the absurdity of human self-deception, with literal masks as its central dramatic symbol and with purposively obvious manipulation of the theatrical environment, and appropriately subtitled "A Clown Show"), the children at Blackfriars could justifiably say, "We shall increase the distance that separates us—a distance that is basic—by our pomp, our manners, our insolence—for we are also [child] actors."[19]

When the Company of His Majesty's Servants appropriated the play for production at the Globe, its managers ostensibly commissioned Webster to write the Induction "to abridge the not-received custom of music" in the public theater; but its main function, it would seem, was to enable the adult actors to create the distance necessary to convey the meaning of *The Malcontent* and which the child actors created so easily by nature. By acknowledging and even emphasizing the physical properties of the playhouse and of the stage, by introducing in their own persons the actors who will in a few moments appear in their respective roles (or masks), by having the actors—representing both actors and spectators—discuss the nature of the play itself and its theatrical history, and by setting a comic mood, Webster's Induction strikingly calls attention to Marston's play as a play and carefully prepares the spectators for the strange, melodramatic, and essentially comic world that is about to be unfolded before them. For them to realize the extent of the play's unreality is for them to grasp that much more its real meaning; the measure of their laughter (and ours) is the measure of their (and our) civilized humanity.

M. L. WINE

Pomona College

[19] See Jean Genet, *The Blacks: A Clown Show*, trans. Bernard Frechtman (New York, 1960), p. 22.

THE MALCONTENT

BENIAMINO IONSONIO,
POETÆ ELEGANTISSIMO, GRAVISSIMO,

AMICO SVO, CANDIDO ET CORDATO,
IOHANNES MARSTON, MVSARVM ALVMNVS,
ASPERAM HANC SVAM THALIAM D.D.

1. BENIAMINO] *Q1–2;* BENIAMINI *Q.*

Dedication.] To Benjamin Jonson, the most discriminating and weighty poet, his frank and sincere friend, John Marston, disciple of the Muses, gives and dedicates this his unpolished comedy.

To the Reader

I am an ill orator, and, in truth, use to indite more honestly than eloquently; for it is my custom to speak as I think, and write as I speak.

In plainness, therefore, understand that in some things I have willingly erred, as in supposing a Duke of Genoa (5) and in taking names different from that city's families: for which some may wittily accuse me, but my defense shall be as honest as many reproofs unto me have been most malicious since, I heartily protest, it was my care to write so far from reasonable offense that even strangers (10) in whose state I laid my scene should not from thence draw any disgrace to any, dead or living. Yet, in despite of my endeavors, I understand some have been most unadvisedly overcunning in misinterpreting me, and with subtlety as deep as hell have maliciously spread ill rumors, which, (15) springing from themselves, might to themselves have heavily returned. Surely I desire to satisfy every firm spirit, who, in all his actions, proposeth to himself no more ends than God and virtue do, whose intentions are always simple: to such I protest that, with my free understanding, (20) I have not glanced at disgrace of any but of those whose unquiet studies labor innovation, contempt of holy policy, reverent, comely superiority, and establish'd unity. For the rest of my supposed tartness, I fear not but unto every worthy mind it will be approved so general and honest as (25) may modestly pass with the freedom of a satire. I would fain leave the paper; only one thing afflicts me, to think that scenes invented merely to be spoken should be enforcively published to be read, and that the least hurt I can receive is to do myself the wrong. But, since others otherwise (30) would do me more, the least inconvenience is to be accepted. I have myself, therefore, set forth this comedy,

14. subtlety] *Q1–2* (*subtilty*); subtilitie *Q*.

---

7. *wittily*] ingeniously.
22. *labor*] labor for.
22. *innovation*] disorder.
28. *merely*] only.
28–29. *enforcively*] by compulsion.

but so that my enforced absence must much rely upon the printer's discretion; but I shall entreat slight errors in orthography may be as slightly overpassed and that the 35 unhandsome shape which this trifle in reading presents may be pardoned for the pleasure it once afforded you when it was presented with the soul of lively action.

Sine aliqua dementia nullus Phoebus.

I. M.

39.] *Me mea sequentur fata. Q1.*

33. *so*] in such a way.
35. *slightly*] inattentively.
39. *Sine . . . Phoebus*] "No poet is without some madness."

Dramatis Personæ

GIOVANNI ALTOFRONTO, disguised MALEVOLE, *sometime Duke of Genoa*
PIETRO JACOMO, *Duke of Genoa*
MENDOZA, *a minion to the Duchess of Pietro Jacomo*
CELSO, *a friend to Altofront* 5
BILIOSO, *an old choleric marshal*
PREPASSO, *a gentleman usher*
FERNEZE, *a young courtier, and enamored on the Duchess*
FERRARDO, *a minion to Duke Pietro Jacomo*
EQUATO, GUERRINO } *two courtiers* 10
AURELIA, *Duchess to Duke Pietro Jacomo*
MARIA, *Duchess to Duke Altofront*
EMILIA, BIANCHA } *two ladies attending the Duchess* [*Aurelia*] 15
MAQUERELLE, *an old pand'ress*
PASSARELLO, *fool to Bilioso*
[CAPTAIN, *guarding the Citadel*
MERCURY, *in the Masque*
SUITORS 20
PAGES
GUARDS

WILLIAM SLY, JOHN SINKLO, RICHARD BURBAGE, HENRY CONDELL, JOHN LOWIN, A TIREMAN] } *Members of the Company of His Majesty's Servants in the Induction* 25

19. PASSARELLO] *addition Q.*

Dramatis Personæ.] Many of the Italianate name tags are obviously descriptive, e.g., Malevole (malevolent), Altofronto (high forehead).
4. *minion*] lover.

THE INDUCTION TO THE MALCONTENT
And the Additions Acted by the King's Majesty's Servants

Written by John Webster

Enter Will Sly, *a* Tireman *following him with a stool.*

TIREMAN.

Sir, the gentlemen will be angry if you sit here.

SLY.

Why? We may sit upon the stage at the private house. Thou dost not take me for a country gentleman, dost? Dost think I fear hissing? I'll hold my life thou took'st me for one of the players. 5

TIREMAN.

No, sir.

SLY.

By God's slid, if you had, I would have given you but sixpence for your stool. Let them that have stale suits sit in the galleries. Hiss at me! He that will be laugh'd out of a tavern or an ordinary shall seldom feed well or be 10 drunk in good company. —Where's Harry Condell, Dick

---

0.1. *Sly*] actor and later shareholder in the King's Men's company until his death in 1608.

0.1. *Tireman*] property or wardrobe man.

2. *the private house*] the Blackfriars theater, where *The Malcontent* originally was performed; the Induction takes place on the outer stage of the public theater, the Globe.

4. *Dost . . . fear hissing?*] alluding to the taunts of the groundlings in the public theater who objected to the gallants who sat on the stage and blocked the action. Dekker, in *The Guls Horne-booke* (London, 1609), advises his gull to sit upon the stage even "though the Scar-crowes in the yard hoot at you, hisse at you, spit at you, yea, throw durt even in your teeth."

7. *slid*] eyelid.

8. *sixpence for your stool*] "By sitting on the stage, you may . . . have a good stoole for sixpence" (Dekker).

8. *stale*] no longer fashionable.

10. *ordinary*] an eating house.

11. *Condell*] associated with the King's Men until his death in 1627; with John Heminges, editor of the First Folio of Shakespeare in 1623.

Burbage, and Will Sly? Let me speak with some of them.

TIREMAN.

An't please you to go in, sir, you may.

SLY.

I tell you, no. I am one that hath seen this play often, and can give them intelligence for their action. I have most of 15 the jests here in my table-book.

Enter Sinklo.

SINKLO.

Save you, coz!

SLY.

O, cousin, come, you shall sit between my legs here.

SINKLO.

No, indeed, cousin; the audience then will take me for a viol-de-gamba, and think that you play upon me. 20

SLY.

Nay, rather that I work upon you, coz.

SINKLO.

We stayed for you at supper last night at my cousin Honeymoon's, the woolen draper. After supper we drew cuts for a score of apricocks, the longest cut still to draw an apricock. By this light 'twas Mistress Frank Honeymoon's 25 fortune still to have the longest cut; I did measure for the women. —What be these, coz?

---

12. *Burbage*] the most distinguished member of the King's Men, upon whose death on March 13, 1619, "the city and the stage were shrouded in gloom" (Edwin Nungezer, *A Dictionary of Actors* [New Haven, 1929], p. 73).

12. *Sly*] who is obviously not acting *in propria persona.*

13. *An't*] If it.

15. *intelligence*] information.

16. *table-book*] pocket notebook.

16.1. *Sinklo*] or Sincler, a relatively undistinguished member of the King's Men; conjectured to be possibly only a hired man, whose role was as a supernumerary (Nungezer, p. 326).

17. *coz*] friend.

22. *stayed*] waited.

23–24. *drew cuts*] a *double entendre* on the practice of drawing as lots straws of various lengths.

24. *apricocks*] apricots.

24. *still*] always.

Enter Dick Burbage, Harry Condell, John Lowin.

SLY.

The players. —God save you!

BURBAGE.

You are very welcome.

SLY.

I pray you, know this gentleman, my cousin; 'tis Master 30
Doomsday's son, the usurer.

CONDELL.

I beseech you, sir, be covered.

SLY.

No, in good faith, for mine ease. Look you, my hat's the
handle to this fan. God's so, what a beast was I, I did not
leave my feather at home. Well, but I'll take an order with 35
you.

Puts his feather in his pocket.

BURBAGE.

Why do you conceal your feather, sir?

SLY.

Why? Do you think I'll have jests broken upon me in the
play, to be laugh'd at? This play hath beaten all your
gallants out of the feathers: Blackfriars hath almost spoil'd 40
Blackfriars for feathers.

SINKLO.

God's so, I thought 'twas for somewhat our gentlewomen at
home counsel'd me to wear my feather to the play; yet I am
loath to spoil it.

35. feather] *Dodsley;* father *Q.*

27.1. Lowin] "Evidently he joined the King's company as a hired man. . . . Through a long life he continued with the King's men, ultimately becoming one of the most prominent members of the company" (Nungezer, p. 239).

32. *be covered*] put your hat on.

34. *handle to this fan*] i.e., the feather (fan) is so large that the hat seems but a handle to it.

34. *God's so*] perversion of *Catzo*, an Italian obscenity.

39–41. *This play . . . feathers*] cf. V.iii.39, where it is declared that the satire of this passage has ruined the feather trade carried on in the Blackfriars district.

42. *for somewhat*] for some purpose.

44. *loath to spoil it*] "by pocketing it" (Spencer).

SLY.

Why, coz? 45

SINKLO.

Because I got it in the tiltyard. There was a herald broke my pate for taking it up; but I have worn it up and down the Strand, and met him forty times since, and yet he dares not challenge it.

SLY.

Do you hear, sir? This play is a bitter play. 50

CONDELL.

Why, sir, 'tis neither satire nor moral, but the mean passage of a history; yet there are a sort of discontented creatures that bear a stingless envy to great ones, and these will wrest the doings of any man to their base, malicious applyment. But should their interpretation come to the test, like 55 your marmoset they presently turn their teeth to their tail and eat it.

SLY.

I will not go so far with you; but I say, any man that hath wit may censure if he sit in the twelvepenny room; and I say again, the play is bitter. 60

BURBAGE.

Sir, you are like a patron that, presenting a poor scholar to a benefice, enjoins him not to rail against anything that stands within compass of his patron's folly. Why should not we enjoy the ancient freedom of poesy? Shall we protest to the ladies that their painting makes them angels? or to 65 my young gallant that his expense in the brothel shall gain him reputation? No, sir, such vices as stand not accountable

---

46. *Because . . . tiltyard*] "The courtly combatants at tilting wore plumes in their helmets which were often shorn off in the contest" (Harrison).

47. *pate*] head. 51. *mean*] ordinary.

54–55. *applyment*] application, interpretation.

56–57. *marmoset . . . eat it*] "this seems a confused recollection of the beaver's supposed habit, when hunted for its stones, of biting them off itself (cf. Pliny [*Naturalis Historia*] xxxii.3)" (Lucas).

59. *censure*] criticize.

59. *twelvepenny room*] box adjoining the stage, where a more "fashionable" playgoer might choose to sit.

to law should be cured as men heal tetters, by casting ink upon them. Would you be satisfied in anything else, sir?

SLY.

Ay, marry, would I: I would know how you came by this play? 70

CONDELL.

Faith, sir, the book was lost; and, because 'twas pity so good a play should be lost, we found it and play it.

SLY.

I wonder you would play it, another company having interest in it. 75

CONDELL.

Why not Malevole in folio with us, as Jeronimo in decimo-sexto with them? They taught us a name for our play; we call it *One for Another.*

SLY.

What are your additions?

BURBAGE.

Sooth, not greatly needful: only as your sallet to your great feast, to entertain a little more time, and to abridge the not-received custom of music in our theater. I must leave you, sir. *Exit* Burbage. 80

SINKLO.

Doth he play the Malcontent?

CONDELL.

Yes, sir. 85

SINKLO.

I durst lay four of mine ears the play is not so well acted as it hath been.

---

68. *tetters*] eruptions of the skin.
70. *marry*] oath, implying surprise.
76–77. *Why not . . . them?*] "Why should not one of our adult actors act the part of Malevole when one of the Blackfriars' boys acted the part of our Jeronimo?" Since the King's Men did not own *The Spanish Tragedy* (of which Hieronimo is the central figure), the play referred to is sometimes taken to be *The First Part of Jeronimo.*
80. *sallet*] salad.
81–82. *to abridge . . . theater*] see Introduction, pp. xxiv–xxv.

CONDELL.

O, no, sir, nothing *ad Parmenonis suem.*

LOWIN.

Have you lost your ears, sir, that you are so prodigal of laying them? 90

SINKLO.

Why did you ask that, friend?

LOWIN.

Marry, sir, because I have heard of a fellow would offer to lay a hundred pound wager that was not worth five baubees; and in this kind you might venture four of your elbows. Yet God defend your coat should have so many! 95

SINKLO.

Nay, truly, I am no great censurer; and yet I might have been one of the College of Critics once. My cousin here hath an excellent memory, indeed, sir.

SLY.

Who? I? I'll tell you a strange thing of myself; and I can tell you, for one that never studied the art of memory, 'tis 100 very strange too.

CONDELL.

What's that, sir?

SLY.

Why, I'll lay a hundred pound I'll walk but once down by the Goldsmiths' Row in Cheap, take notice of the signs, and tell you them with a breath instantly. 105

LOWIN.

'Tis very strange.

---

88. *ad Parmenonis suem*] compared with Parmeno's pig. "Parmeno (according to Plutarch *Symposiaca problemata* V.i.) could imitate the grunting of a pig so well that, when a genuine pig was privily introduced into competition with him, his admirers still cried, 'Nothing to Parmeno's pig!'" (Wood). Condell is rebuking Sinklo for holding to an opinion which has no basis in fact: that the boys acted the play better than the men will.

89. *lost your ears*] "with insolent allusion to the ear-cropping of felons" (Lucas).

93. *baubees*] "A Scotch coin . . . in modern use, a halfpenny" (*OED*); possibly an allusion to the needy followers of King James I.

95. *defend*] forbid. 96. *censurer*] judge.

104. *Cheap*] Cheapside, the old Market Place of London.

SLY.

They begin as the world did, with Adam and Eve. There's in all just five and fifty. I do use to meditate much when I come to plays too. What do you think might come into a man's head now, seeing all this company? 110

CONDELL.

I know not, sir.

SLY.

I have an excellent thought: if some fifty of the Grecians that were cramm'd in the horse-belly had eaten garlic, do you not think the Trojans might have smelt out their knavery? 115

CONDELL.

Very likely.

SLY.

By God, I would they had, for I love Hector horribly.

SINKLO.

O, but, coz, coz!—
"Great Alexander, when he came to the tomb of Achilles,
Spake with a big loud voice, 'O thou thrice blessed and happy!'" 120

SLY.

Alexander was an ass to speak so well of a filthy cullion.

LOWIN.

Good sir, will you leave the stage? I'll help you to a private room.

SLY.

Come, coz, let's take some tobacco. —Have you never a prologue? 125

117. they] *Dyce;* he *Q*.

---

108. *five and fifty*] In his *Survey of London* (1598), Stow cites "ten fair dwelling-houses and fourteen shops."

112. *excellent thought*] "a hit at the groundlings: being obviously suggested to Sly's mind by the reek of garlic rising from them" (Lucas).

119–120. *Great . . . happy*] the way Sinklo remembers John Harvey's hexameter translation of Petrarch's sonnet CLIII, reproduced by Gabriel Harvey in a letter to the poet Spenser (*Three Proper, and wittie, familiar Letters*, 1580).

121. *cullion*] rascal. Alexander exclaimed ll. 119–120 while paying homage at the tomb of Achilles.

123. *room*] i.e., the twelvepenny box.

LOWIN.

Not any, sir.

SLY.

Let me see, I will make one extempore. Come to them and, fencing of a congee with arms and legs, be round with them:

Gentlemen, I could wish for the women's sakes you had all soft cushions; and, gentlewomen, I could wish that for the men's sakes you had all more easy standings. 130

What would they wish more but the play now? And that they shall have instantly. [*Exeunt.*]

127–129. *Come . . . them*] *Q; Dyce, at the suggestion of J. P. Collier, and other editors print these lines as stage directions.*

134. S.D.] *Dyce.*

The Malcontent

Vexat censura columbas.

An Imperfect Ode, Being But One Staff, Spoken by the

PROLOGUE

To wrest each hurtless thought to private sense
Is the foul use of ill-bred Impudence:
Immodest censure now grows wild,
All overrunning.
Let Innocence be ne'er so chaste, 5
Yet at the last
She is defil'd
With too nice-brained cunning.
O you of fairer soul,
Control 10
With an *Herculean* arm
This harm;
And once teach all old freedom of a pen,
Which still must write of fools, whiles't writes of men!

[I.i] *The vilest out-of-tune music being heard, enter* Bilioso *and* Prepasso.

BILIOSO.
Why, how now! Are ye mad, or drunk, or both, or what?

PREPASSO.
Are ye building Babylon there?

BILIOSO.
Here's a noise in court! You think you are in a tavern, do you not?

censura] *Q, Q1; censuræ Q2.*
PROLOGUE] *follows conclusion of play in Q, the Epilogue in Q2; not in Q1.*

0.1. *Vexat censura columbas*] "Censorship disturbs the doves."
0.2. *Staff*] Stanza. 3. *Immodest*] Immoderate.

[I.i]
2. *Babylon*] with pun on Babel.

PREPASSO.

You think you are in a brothel house, do you not? —This room is ill-scented. 5

Enter One with a perfume.

So, perfume, perfume; some upon me, I pray thee. —The Duke is upon instant entrance; so, make place there!

[I.ii]

Enter the Duke Pietro, Ferrardo, Count Equato, Count Celso *before, and* Guerrino.

PIETRO.

Where breathes that music?

BILIOSO.

The discord rather than the music is heard from the malcontent Malevole's chamber.

FERRARDO [*calling*].

Malevole!

MALEVOLE (*out of his chamber*).

Yaugh, God o' man, what dost thou there? Duke's Ganymede, Juno's jealous of thy long stockings. Shadow of a woman, what wouldst, weasel? Thou lamb o' court, what dost thou bleat for? Ah, you smooth-chinn'd catamite! 5

PIETRO.

Come down, thou ragged cur, and snarl here. I give thy dogged sullenness free liberty; trot about and bespurtle whom thou pleasest. 10

MALEVOLE.

I'll come among you, you goatish-blooded toderers, as

4. S.D.] *Dyce.* 9. ragged] *Q;* rugged *Q1–2.*

---

8. *instant*] immediate.

[I.ii]

5. S.D. *out . . . chamber*] probably on upper stage; cf. l. 9 ("Come down").

5. *o'*] of. 5–6. *Ganymede*] Jupiter's cupbearer. 7. *lamb*] favorite.

8. *catamite*] male prostitute ("corrupt form of *Ganymēdes* name of Jupiter's cupbearer," *OED*).

10. *bespurtle*] bespatter, abuse. 12. *goatish-blooded*] lustful.

12. *toderers*] Steevens conjectures that the word is coined from *tod*, a weight in the wool trade; hence, a toderer is a dealer in sheep, i.e., a male prostitute.

gum into taffeta, to fret, to fret. I'll fall like a sponge into water to suck up, to suck up. Howl again! I'll go to church and come to you. [*Exit above.*] 15

PIETRO.

This Malevole is one of the most prodigious affections that ever convers'd with nature: a man, or rather a monster, more discontent than Lucifer when he was thrust out of the presence. His appetite is unsatiable as the grave, as far from any content as from heaven. His highest delight is to pro- 20 cure others' vexation, and therein he thinks he truly serves heaven; for 'tis his position, whosoever in this earth can be contented is a slave and damn'd; therefore does he afflict all in that to which they are most affected. Th' elements struggle within him; his own soul is at variance within her- 25 self; his speech is halter-worthy at all hours. I like him; faith, he gives good intelligence to my spirit, makes me understand those weaknesses which others' flattery palliates. Hark! they sing.

[*A Song.*]

[I.iii] *Enter* Malevole *after the song.*

PIETRO.

See, he comes. Now shall you hear the extremity of a malcontent: he is as free as air; he blows over every man. —And, sir, whence come you now?

14. I'll go to church] *Q*, *Q2;* I'll pray *Q1*.
15. S.D.] *Dyce*.
25–26. within herself] *addition Q*.
29.1. *A Song*] *Dyce*.
[I.iii]
1. S.P. PIETRO.] *Dodsley; not in Qq*.

13. *gum into taffeta*] inferior taffeta was stiffened with gum, which caused it to fray.
13. *fret*] to irritate, with pun on *fray*.
16. *prodigious affections*] persons of enormous passions.
24. *affected*] inclined.
26. *halter-worthy*] deserving to be hanged.
29.1. *A Song*] In *The English Dramatic Lyric, 1603–42* (New Haven, 1951), W. R. Bowden suggests that the songs for which no text or indication is given were simply selected from the permanent repertoire of the boys' companies and the tunes withheld from publication so that they did not grow old (see especially pp. 91, 93).

MALEVOLE.

From the public place of much dissimulation, the church.

PIETRO.

What didst there? 5

MALEVOLE.

Talk with a usurer; take up at interest.

PIETRO.

I wonder what religion thou art of.

MALEVOLE.

Of a soldier's religion.

PIETRO.

And what dost think makes most infidels now?

MALEVOLE.

Sects, sects. I have seen seeming Piety change her robe so 10
oft that sure none but some arch-devil can shape her a new petticoat.

PIETRO.

O, a religious policy.

MALEVOLE.

But damnation on a politic religion! I am weary. Would I were one of the Duke's hounds now. 15

PIETRO.

But what's the common news abroad, Malevole? Thou dogg'st rumor still.

MALEVOLE.

Common news? Why, common words are, "God save ye," "Fare ye well"; common actions, flattery and cozenage; common things, women and cuckolds. —And how does my 20
little Ferrard? Ah, ye lecherous animal!—my little ferret, he goes sucking up and down the palace into every hen's nest, like a weasel—and to what dost thou addict thy time to now more than to those antique painted drabs that

4. the church] *Q, but deleted from many copies; omitted entirely from Q2; in Q1, but deleted from all but two of ten extant copies.*
7. of] *Q; not in Q1–2.*
11. new] *Q1–2; not in Q.*
13. O] *Qq (corrected);* Of *Q1 (uncorrected).*
14–15. I . . . now] *Q, Q2; not in Q1.*

---

6. *take up*] borrow. 19. *cozenage*] deception. 24. *drabs*] strumpets.

are still affected of young courtiers, Flattery, Pride, and Venery? 25

FERRARDO.

I study languages. Who dost think to be the best linguist of our age?

MALEVOLE.

Phew, the devil. Let him possess thee; he'll teach thee to speak all languages most readily and strangely; and great 30 reason, marry, he's travel'd greatly in the world and is everywhere.

FERRARDO.

Save i' th' court.

MALEVOLE.

Ay, save i' th' court. —(*To* Bilioso.) And how dost my old muckhill, overspread with fresh snow? Thou half a man, 35 half a goat, all a beast! How does thy young wife, old huddle?

BILIOSO.

Out, you improvident rascal!

MALEVOLE.

Do, kick, thou hugely-horn'd old duke's ox, good Master Make-please. 40

PIETRO.

How dost thou live nowadays, Malevole?

MALEVOLE.

Why, like the knight, Sir Patrick Penlolians, with killing o' spiders for my lady's monkey.

PIETRO.

How dost spend the night? I hear thou never sleep'st.

40. Make-please] *Qq* (*Make-pleece*); Make-pleas *Dyce;* Make-peace *Dodsley.*

42. Penlolians] *Q*, *Q2*; Penlohans *Q1* (*corrected*); Penlobrans *Q1* (*uncorrected*).

---

25. *affected of*] desired by.

29–32. *Phew . . . everywhere*] "an allusion to the old superstition . . . that a person possessed by the devil was able to converse in various tongues" (Bullen).

37. *huddle*] "miserly old fellow" (*OED*).

40. *Make-please*] flatterer.

42. *Sir Patrick Penlolians*] unidentified.

MALEVOLE.

O, no, but dream the most fantastical! O heaven! O fubbery, fubbery! 45

PIETRO.

Dream! What dream'st?

MALEVOLE.

Why, methinks I see that signior pawn his footcloth, that *metreza* her plate; this madam takes physic that t'other *monsieur* may minister to her. Here is a pander jewel'd; there 50 is a fellow in shift of satin this day that could not shift a shirt t'other night. Here a Paris supports that Helen; there's a Lady Guinevere bears up that Sir Lancelot. Dreams, dreams, visions, fantasies, chimeras, imaginations, tricks, conceits! —(*To* Prepasso.) Sir Tristram Trimtram, 55 come aloft, Jackanapes, with a whim-wham. Here's a knight of the land of Catito shall play at trap with any page in Europe, do the sword dance with any morris dancer in Christendom, ride at the ring till the fin of his eyes look as blue as the welkin, and run the wild-goose chase even 60 with Pompey the Huge.

PIETRO.

You run!

MALEVOLE.

To the devil. —Now, Signior Guerrino, that thou from a most pitied prisoner shouldst grow a most loath'd flatterer!

51. is] *Q; not in Q1–2.* 63.] Guerchino *Qq.*

46. *fubbery*] deception.
48. *footcloth*] adorned trappings of a horse.
49. *metreza*] mistress (Italian). 49. *t'other*] that other.
53. *Lady Guinevere*] "applicable to any lady of easy manners" (Halliwell).
55. *conceits*] fancies.
55–56. *Sir Tristram . . . Jackanapes*] the cry of an ape-trainer to persuade his apes to perform; *jackanapes* also means fool, coxcomb.
56. *whim-wham*] whimsy (B-P).
57. *land of Catito*] Spencer refers to his correspondence with Professor Kittredge: "'Catito' is a coinage from 'cat', which (like 'trap') is the name of a boyish game. 'Catito' = sport-land, boys' play-land."
57. *trap*] "A game played with a ball, a bat, and a wooden trap" (Neilson).
59. *ride at the ring*] a sport in which a rider attempted to thrust his spear or lance through a suspended ring.
59. *fin*] lid. 60. *welkin*] sky.

—Alas, poor Celso, thy star's oppress'd: thou art an honest lord. 'Tis pity. 65

EQUATO.

Is't pity?

MALEVOLE.

Ay, marry, is't, philosophical Equato; and 'tis pity that thou, being so excellent a scholar by art, shouldst be so ridiculous a fool by nature. —I have a thing to tell you, duke; bid 'em avaunt, bid 'em avaunt. 70

PIETRO.

Leave us, leave us.

Exeunt all saving Pietro *and* Malevole.

Now, sir, what is't?

MALEVOLE.

Duke, thou art a *becco*, a *cornuto*.

PIETRO.

How? 75

MALEVOLE.

Thou art a cuckold.

PIETRO.

Speak; unshale him quick.

MALEVOLE.

With most tumbler-like nimbleness.

PIETRO.

Who? By whom? I burst with desire.

MALEVOLE.

Mendoza is the man makes thee a horn'd beast; duke, 'tis Mendoza cornutes thee. 80

PIETRO.

What conformance? Relate; short, short!

MALEVOLE.

As a lawyer's beard.

There is an old crone in the court—her name is Maquerelle;

72.1.] *after* is't? (*l. 73*) Q.

---

65. *oppress'd*] in the descendant.
74. *becco*] cuckold (Italian).
74. *cornuto*] horned one, i.e., a cuckold (Italian).
77. *unshale*] unshell, i.e., reveal.
82. *conformance*] confirmation. 84. *crone*] withered old woman.

She is my mistress, sooth to say, and she doth ever tell me. 85
Blurt o' rhyme, blurt o' rhyme! Maquerelle is a cunning bawd; I am an honest villain; thy wife is a close drab; and thou art a notorious cuckold. Farewell, duke.

PIETRO.

Stay, stay.

MALEVOLE.

Dull, dull duke, can lazy patience make lame revenge? O 90
God, for a woman to make a man that which God never created, never made!

PIETRO.

What did God never make?

MALEVOLE.

A cuckold! To be made a thing that's hoodwink'd with kindness whilst every rascal fillips his brows; to have a cox- 95
comb with egregious horns pinn'd to a lord's back, every page sporting himself with delightful laughter, whilst he must be the last must know it. Pistols and poniards! Pistols and poniards!

PIETRO.

Death and damnation! 100

MALEVOLE.

Lightning and thunder!

PIETRO.

Vengeance and torture!

MALEVOLE.

Catzo!

PIETRO.

O, revenge!

MALEVOLE.

Nay, to select among ten thousand fairs 105
A lady far inferior to the most
In fair proportion both of limb and soul;

105–146. Nay . . . think it] *addition Q*.

---

86. *Blurt o'*] a fig for. 87. *close*] secret. 87. *drab*] harlot.
95. *fillips his brows*] alluding to his cuckold's horns.
103. *Catzo*] obscene exclamation of disgust (Italian).

To take her from austerer check of parents,
To make her his by most devoutful rites,
Make her commandress of a better essence 110
Than is the gorgeous world, even of a man;
To hug her with as rais'd an appetite
As usurers do their delv'd-up treasury
(Thinking none tells it but his private self);
To meet her spirit in a nimble kiss, 115
Distilling panting ardor to her heart;
True to her sheets, nay, diets strong his blood,
To give her height of hymeneal sweets—

PIETRO.
O God!

MALEVOLE.
Whilst she lisps and gives him some court *quelquechose*, 120
Made only to provoke, not satiate:
And yet, even then, the thaw of her delight
Flows from lewd heat of apprehension,
Only from strange imagination's rankness,
That forms the adulterer's presence in her soul 125
And makes her think she clips the foul knave's loins.

PIETRO.
Affliction to my blood's root!

MALEVOLE.
Nay, think, but think what may proceed of this;
Adultery is often the mother of incest.

PIETRO.
Incest! 130

MALEVOLE.
Yes, incest. Mark! Mendoza of his wife begets perchance a daughter; Mendoza dies; his son marries this daughter. Say you? Nay, 'tis frequent, not only probable, but no question often acted whilst ignorance, fearless ignorance, clasps his own seed. 135

PIETRO.
Hideous imagination!

---

114. *tells*] counts.
120. *quelquechose*] dainty, trifle.
126. *clips*] embraces.

MALEVOLE.

Adultery! Why, next to the sin of simony, 'tis the most horrid transgression under the cope of salvation.

PIETRO.

Next to simony?

MALEVOLE.

Ay, next to simony, in which our men in next age shall not sin. 140

PIETRO.

Not sin? Why?

MALEVOLE.

Because (thanks to some churchmen) our age will leave them nothing to sin with. But adultery—O dullness!—should show exemplary punishment, that intemperate 145 bloods may freeze but to think it. I would dam him and all his generation; my own hands should do it—ha, I would not trust heaven with my vengeance anything.

PIETRO.

Anything, anything, Malevole! Thou shalt see instantly what temper my spirit holds. Farewell; remember I forget 150 thee not; farewell. *Exit* Pietro.

MALEVOLE.

Farewell.
Lean thoughtfulness, a sallow meditation,
Suck thy veins dry! Distemperance rob thy sleep!
The heart's disquiet is revenge most deep: 155
He that gets blood, the life of flesh but spills,
But he that breaks heart's peace, the dear soul kills.—
Well, this disguise doth yet afford me that
Which kings do seldom hear, or great men use—
Free speech; and though my state's usurp'd, 160
Yet this affected strain gives me a tongue
As fetterless as is an emperor's.
I may speak foolishly, ay, knavishly,

145. should show] *Dyce;* shue, should *Q.*

152–169] *addition Q.*

---

138. *cope of salvation*] under heaven.
146. *dam*] choke, stop up (B-H-N).
154. *Distemperance*] referring to the disordering of the "humors."

Always carelessly, yet no one thinks it fashion
To poise my breath; for he that laughs and strikes 165
Is lightly felt, or seldom struck again.
Duke, I'll torment thee: now my just revenge
From thee than crown a richer gem shall part.
Beneath God naught's so dear as a calm heart.

[I.iv] *Enter* Celso.

CELSO.

My honor'd lord—

MALEVOLE.

Peace, speak low; peace! O Celso, constant lord,
Thou to whose faith I only rest discovered,
Thou, one of full ten millions of men,
That lovest virtue only for itself, 5
Thou in whose hands old Ops may put her soul,
Behold forever-banish'd Altofront,
This Genoa's last year's duke. O truly noble!
I wanted those old instruments of state,
Dissemblance and suspect. I could not time it, Celso; 10
My throne stood like a point in middest of a circle,
To all of equal nearness; bore with none;
Reign'd all alike; so slept in fearless virtue,
Suspectless, too suspectless; till the crowd,
Still lickerous of untried novelties, 15
Impatient with severer government,
Made strong with Florence, banish'd Altofront.

CELSO.

Strong with Florence! Ay, thence your mischief rose,
For when the daughter of the Florentine
Was matched once with this Pietro, now duke, 20

20. this] *Q1–2;* his *Q.*

---

165. *poise my breath*] "ponder seriously over what I am saying."
166. *again*] in return (B-P).
168. *From . . . part*] "shall part from thee a gem richer than a crown."
[I.iv]
6. *Ops*] goddess of plenty. 9. *wanted*] lacked.
10. *suspect*] suspicion. 14. *Suspectless*] unsuspecting.
15. *lickerous*] keenly desirous. 17. *Made strong*] allied.

No stratagem of state untried was left,
Till you of all—

MALEVOLE. Of all was quite bereft.
Alas, Maria too, close prisoned,
My true-faith'd duchess, i' th' citadel!

CELSO.
I'll still adhere; let's mutiny and die. 25

MALEVOLE.
O, no, climb not a falling tower, Celso;
'Tis well held desperation, no zeal,
Hopeless to strive with fate. Peace! Temporize!
Hope, hope, that never forsak'st the wretched'st man,
Yet bidd'st me live and lurk in this disguise! 30
What, play I well the free-breath'd discontent?
Why, man, we are all philosophical monarchs
Or natural fools. Celso, the court's afire;
The duchess' sheets will smoke for't ere it be long.
Impure Mendoza, that sharp-nos'd lord, that made 35
The cursed match link'd Genoa with Florence,
Now broad-horns the duke, which he now knows.
Discord to malcontents is very manna;
When the ranks are burst, then scuffle, Altofront.

CELSO.
Ay, but durst— 40

MALEVOLE.
'Tis gone; 'tis swallow'd like a mineral.
Some way 'twill work. Pheut, I'll not shrink;
He's resolute who can no lower sink.

Bilioso *entering*, Malevole *shifteth his speech.*

MALEVOLE.
O, the father of Maypoles! Did you never see a fellow whose strength consisted in his breath, respect in his office, 45 religion in his lord, and love in himself? Why, then, behold!

26. no] *Q, Q2; not in Q1.*
32–43.] *Dyce; as prose Qq.*
43.1–87.1.] *addition Q.*
46. religion in] *Dyce;* religion on *Q.*

37. *broad-horns*] cuckolds.
41. *mineral*] i.e., mineral medicine; a pill.
42. *Pheut*] exclamation of disgust.

BILIOSO.

Signior—

MALEVOLE.

My right worshipful lord, your court nightcap makes you have a passing high forehead.

BILIOSO.

I can tell you strange news, but I am sure you know them already: the Duke speaks much good of you. 50

MALEVOLE.

Go to, then; and shall you and I now enter into a strict friendship?

BILIOSO.

Second one another?

MALEVOLE.

Yes. 55

BILIOSO.

Do one another good offices?

MALEVOLE.

Just. What though I call'd thee old ox, egregious wittol, broken-bellied coward, rotten mummy? Yet, since I am in favor—

BILIOSO.

Words, of course, terms of disport. His grace presents you by me a chain, as his grateful remembrance for—I am ignorant for what; marry, ye may impart. Yet howsoever—come, dear friend. Dost know my son? 60

MALEVOLE.

Your son?

BILIOSO.

He shall eat woodcocks, dance jigs, make possets, and play at shuttlecock with any young lord about the court. He has as sweet a lady, too. Dost know her little bitch? 65

MALEVOLE.

'Tis a dog, man.

48–49. *your court nightcap . . . forehead*] alluding to his being a cuckold.

57. *wittol*] contented cuckold.

65. *possets*] drinks "composed of hot milk curdled with ale, wine, or other liquor, often with sugar, spices, or other ingredients" (*OED*).

BILIOSO.

Believe me, a she-bitch. O, 'tis a good creature! Thou shalt be her servant. I'll make thee acquainted with my young wife too. What, I keep her not at court for nothing! 'Tis grown to supper time; come to my table—that, anything I have, stands open to thee. 70

MALEVOLE ([*aside*] *to* Celso).

How smooth to him that is in state of grace,
How servile is the rugged'st courtier's face! 75
What profit, nay, what nature would keep down,
Are heav'd to them are minions to a crown.
Envious ambition never sates his thirst,
Till, sucking all, he swells and swells, and bursts.

BILIOSO.

I shall now leave you with my always-best wishes; only let's hold betwixt us a firm correspondence, a mutual friendly-reciprocal kind of steady-unanimous-heartily-leagued— 80

MALEVOLE.

Did your signiorship ne'er see a pigeonhouse that was smooth, round, and white without, and full of holes and stink within? Ha' ye not, old courtier? 85

BILIOSO.

O, yes, 'tis the form, the fashion of them all.

MALEVOLE.

Adieu, my true court friend; farewell, my dear Castilio.

Exit Bilioso.

CELSO.

Yonder's Mendoza. *Descries* Mendoza.

MALEVOLE. True, the privy key.

CELSO.

I take my leave, sweet lord. *Exit* Celso.

MALEVOLE. 'Tis fit; away!

---

77. *them are*] them who are. 77. *minions*] favorites.
81. *correspondence*] amity.
87. *Castilio*] Baldassare Castiglione, whose famous courtesy book was translated into English by Sir Thomas Hoby in 1561 as *The Book of the Courtier*.

[I.v] *Enter* Mendoza *with three or four Suitors.*

MENDOZA.
Leave your suits with me; I can and will. Attend my secretary; leave me. [*Exeunt Suitors.*]

MALEVOLE.
Mendoza, hark ye, hark ye. You are a treacherous villain, God be wi' ye!

MENDOZA.
Out, you baseborn rascal! 5

MALEVOLE.
We are all the sons of heaven, though a tripe-wife were our mother. Ah, you whoreson, hot-rein'd he-marmoset! Ægisthus—didst ever hear of one Ægisthus?

MENDOZA.
Gisthus?

MALEVOLE.
Ay, Ægisthus; he was a filthy, incontinent fleshmonger, 10 such a one as thou art.

MENDOZA.
Out, grumbling rogue!

MALEVOLE.
Orestes, beware Orestes!

MENDOZA.
Out, beggar!

MALEVOLE.
I once shall rise! 15

MENDOZA.
Thou rise?

MALEVOLE.
Ay, at the resurrection.
No vulgar seed but once may rise and shall;
No king so huge but 'fore he die may fall. *Exit.*

2. S.D.] *Dodsley.* *Q1–2.*
4. be wi'] *Dodsley;* bwy *Q;* buye

---

6. *tripe-wife*] woman who sells tripe.
7. *whoreson*] detestable. 7. *hot-rein'd*] lecherous.
8. *Ægisthus*] lover of Clytemnestra who cuckolded Agamemnon; later slain by Agamemnon's son Orestes.

MENDOZA.

Now, good Elysium! what a delicious heaven is it for a man to be in a prince's favor! O sweet God! O pleasure! O fortune! O all thou best of life! What should I think, what say, what do, to be a favorite, a minion? To have a general timorous respect, observe a man, a stateful silence in his presence, solitariness in his absence, a confused hum and busy murmur of obsequious suitors training him, the cloth held up and way proclaimed before him, petitionary vassals licking the pavement with their slavish knees whilst some odd palace-lamprels that engender with snakes, and are full of eyes on both sides, with a kind of insinuated humbleness fix all their delights upon his brow! O blessed state! What a ravishing prospect doth the Olympus of favor yield! Death, I cornute the duke! Sweet women, most sweet ladies, nay, angels! By heaven, he is more accursed than a devil that hates you, or is hated by you, and happier than a god that loves you, or is beloved by you. You preservers of mankind, lifeblood of society, who would live, nay, who can live without you? O paradise, how majestical is your austerer presence! How imperiously chaste is your more modest face! But, O, how full of ravishing attraction is your pretty, petulant, languishing, lasciviously composed countenance! these amorous smiles, those soul-warming sparkling glances, ardent as those flames that sing'd the world by heedless Phaëthon! In body how delicate, in soul how witty, in discourse how pregnant, in life how wary, in favors how judicious, in day how sociable, and in night how—O pleasure unutterable! Indeed, it is most certain, one man cannot deserve only to enjoy a beauteous woman. But a duchess! In despite of Phoebus, I'll write a sonnet instantly in praise of her. *Exit.* 50

30. insinuated] *Q*, *Q2;* insinuating *Q1.*
31. delights] *Q*, *Q2;* lights *Q1.*
43. glances] *Q* (*corrected*); glancet *Q* (*uncorrected*).

24. *observe*] "to treat with ceremonious respect or reverence" (*OED*).
26. *training*] following. 29. *lamprels*] lamprey-like fish.
33. *cornute*] make a cuckold of.
44. *Phaëthon*] who proved unable to guide the horses of the sun and nearly singed the world until Jupiter intervened.
50. *Phoebus*] god of poetry.

[I.vi]

Enter Ferneze *ushering* Aurelia, Emilia *and* Maquerelle *bearing up her train*, Biancha *attending; all go out but* Aurelia, Maquerelle, *and* Ferneze.

AURELIA.

And is't possible? Mendoza slight me! Possible?

FERNEZE.

Possible!
What can be strange in him that's drunk with favor,
Grows insolent with grace? Speak, Maquerelle, speak.

MAQUERELLE.

To speak feelingly, more, more richly in solid sense than worthless words, give me those jewels of your ears to receive my enforced duty. As for my part, 'tis well known I can put up anything (Ferneze *privately feeds* Maquerelle's *hands with jewels during this speech*), can bear patiently with any man: But when I heard he wronged your precious sweetness, I was enforced to take deep offense. 'Tis most certain he loves Emilia with high appetite; and, as she told me (as you know, we women impart our secrets one to another), when she repulsed his suit, in that he was possessed with your endeared grace, Mendoza most ingratefully renounced all faith to you. 5 10 15

FERNEZE.

Nay, call'd you—speak, Maquerelle, speak.

MAQUERELLE.

By heaven, "witch," "dried biscuit," and contested blushlessly he lov'd you but for a spurt or so.

FERNEZE.

For maintenance. 20

MAQUERELLE.

Advancement and regard.

AURELIA.

O villain! O impudent Mendoza!

3. with favor] Q *(corrected); not in* Q *(uncorrected)*.
8. up] *Q1; not in* Q, *Q2*.
18. biscuit] *Q1* (*bisquet*)*;* bisque Q, *Q2*.

7–8. *put up*] endure.

MAQUERELLE.

Nay, he is the rustiest-jaw'd, the foulest-mouth'd knave in railing against our sex; he will rail against women—

AURELIA.

How? how? 25

MAQUERELLE.

I am asham'd to speak't, I.

AURELIA.

I love to hate him—speak.

MAQUERELLE.

Why, when Emilia scorn'd his base unsteadiness, the black-throated rascal scolded and said—

AURELIA.

What? 30

MAQUERELLE.

Troth, 'tis too shameless.

AURELIA.

What said he?

MAQUERELLE.

Why, that at four women were fools; at fourteen, drabs; at forty, bawds; at fourscore, witches; and at a hundred, cats. 35

AURELIA.

O unlimitable impudency!

FERNEZE.

But, as for poor Ferneze's fixed heart,
Was never shadeless meadow drier parch'd
Under the scorching heat of heaven's dog
Than is my heart with your enforcing eyes. 40

MAQUERELLE.

A hot simile!

FERNEZE.

Your smiles have been my heaven, your frowns my hell.
O, pity, then! Grace should with beauty dwell.

23. jaw'd] *Q1–2* (*iawde*); iade *Q*.
24. against] *Q*; agen *Q1–2*.
34. at a] *Dodsley*; a *Qq*.
34. hundred] *Q*; hundredth *Q1–2*.

23. *rustiest-*] rudest-.
39. *heaven's dog*] the Dog Star ("ascendant in July and August," Harrison).
40. *enforcing*] compelling, ravishing.

MAQUERELLE.

Reasonable perfect, by'r Lady.

AURELIA.

I will love thee, be it but in despite 45
Of that Mendoza. "Witch," Ferneze, "witch"!
Ferneze, thou art the duchess' favorite;
Be faithful, private; but 'tis dangerous.

FERNEZE.

His love is liveless that for love fears breath;
The worst that's due to sin, O, would 'twere death! 50

AURELIA.

Enjoy my favor. I will be sick instantly and take physic; therefore, in depth of night visit—

MAQUERELLE.

Visit her chamber, but conditionally: You shall not offend her bed, by this diamond!

FERNEZE.

By this diamond. *Gives it to* Maquerelle. 55

MAQUERELLE.

Nor tarry longer than you please, by this ruby!

FERNEZE.

By this ruby. *Gives again.*

MAQUERELLE.

And that the door shall not creak.

FERNEZE.

And that the door shall not creak.

MAQUERELLE.

Nay, but swear. 60

FERNEZE.

By this purse. *Gives her his purse.*

MAQUERELLE.

Go to, I'll keep your oaths for you. Remember, visit.

Enter Mendoza, *reading a sonnet.*

AURELIA.

"Dried biscuit!" —Look where the base wretch comes.

57. S.D.] *Q, Q2; not in Q1.*
60. S.P. MAQUERELLE] Dodsley; *speech assigned to Malevole Qq.*
61. S.D.] *Q, Q2; not in Q1.*

MENDOZA.

"Beauty's life, heaven's model, love's queen"—

MAQUERELLE [*aside*].

That's his Emilia. 65

MENDOZA.

"Nature's triumph, best on earth"—

MAQUERELLE [*aside*].

Meaning Emilia.

MENDOZA.

"Thou only wonder that the world hath seen"—

MAQUERELLE [*aside*].

That's Emilia.

AURELIA [*aside*].

Must I then hear her prais'd?—Mendoza! 70

MENDOZA.

Madam, your excellency is graciously encounter'd; I have been writing passionate flashes in honor of— *Exit* Ferneze.

AURELIA.

Out, villain, villain! O judgment, where have been my eyes? What bewitched election made me dote on thee? What sorcery made me love thee? But, be gone; bury thy 75 head. O, that I could do more than loathe thee! Hence, worst of ill: No reason ask; our reason is our will.

Exit with Maquerelle.

MENDOZA.

Women! Nay, furies; nay, worse; for they torment only the bad, but women good and bad. Damnation of mankind! Breath, hast thou prais'd them for this? And is't you, 80 Ferneze, are wriggled into smock-grace? Sit sure. O, that I could rail against these monsters in nature, models of hell, curse of the earth, women that dare attempt anything, and what they attempt they care not how they accomplish; without all premeditation or prevention; rash in asking, 85

66. on] *Q*, *Q2*; of *Q1*. 77. ask] *Q*; else *Q1–2*.

81. *smock-grace*] intimate favor (B-P).
85. *prevention*] precaution.

desperate in working, impatient in suffering, extreme in desiring, slaves unto appetite, mistresses in dissembling, only constant in unconstancy, only perfect in counterfeiting; their words are feigned, their eyes forged, their sights dissembled, their looks counterfeit, their hair false, their given hopes deceitful, their very breath artificial. Their blood is their only god; bad clothes and old age are only the devils they tremble at. That I could rail now! 90

[I.vii] *Enter* Pietro, *his sword drawn.*

PIETRO.
A mischief fill thy throat, thou foul-jaw'd slave!
Say thy prayers.

MENDOZA. I ha' forgot 'em.

PIETRO. Thou shalt die!

MENDOZA.
So shalt thou. I am heart-mad.

PIETRO. I am horn-mad.

MENDOZA.
Extreme mad.

PIETRO. Monstrously mad.

MENDOZA. Why?

PIETRO.
Why? Thou, thou hast dishonored my bed. 5

MENDOZA.
I? Come, come, sit; here's my bare heart to thee,
As steady as is this center to the glorious world.
And yet, hark, thou art a *cornuto*—but by me?

PIETRO.
Yes, slave, by thee.

7. the] *Q, Q2;* this *Q1.*

---

89. *sights*] sighs.
[I.vii]
3. *horn-mad*] extremely mad, with pun on *horns.*
7. *center*] earth, center of the Ptolemaic universe.

MENDOZA.

Do not, do not with tart and spleenful breath 10
Lose him can lose thee. I offend my duke?
Bear record, O ye dumb and raw-air'd nights,
How vigilant my sleepless eyes have been
To watch the traitor! Record, thou spirit of truth,
With what debasement I ha' thrown myself 15
To under offices, only to learn
The truth, the party, time, the means, the place,
By whom, and when, and where thou wert disgrac'd!
And am I paid with "slave"? Hath my intrusion
To places private and prohibited, 20
Only to observe the closer passages—
Heaven knows with vows of revelation—
Made me suspected, made me deem'd a villain?
What rogue hath wronged us?

PIETRO. Mendoza, I may err.

MENDOZA.

Err? 'Tis too mild a name; but err and err, 25
Run giddy with suspect 'fore through me thou know
That which most creatures, save thyself, do know.
Nay, since my service hath so loath'd reject,
'Fore I'll reveal, shalt find them clipp'd together.

PIETRO.

Mendoza, thou know'st I am a most plain-breasted man. 30

MENDOZA.

The fitter to make a cuckold! Would your brows were most plain too!

PIETRO.

Tell me; indeed, I heard thee rail.

MENDOZA.

At women, true. Why, what cold phlegm could choose,

31. cuckold] *Q*, *Q2;* Cornuto *Q1.*

---

10. *spleenful*] passionate, irritable. 16. *under offices*] menial tasks.
21. *closer passages*] more secret occurrences.
28. *reject*] rejection. 29. *clipp'd*] embraced.
34. *phlegm*] "one of the four bodily 'humors', cold and moist, and supposed when predominant to cause constitutional indolence or apathy" (*OED*).

Knowing a lord so honest, virtuous, 35
So boundless-loving, bounteous, fair-shap'd, sweet,
To be contemn'd, abus'd, defam'd, made cuckold?
Heart! I hate all women for't: sweet sheets, wax lights, antique bedposts, cambric smocks, villainous curtains, arras pictures, oil'd hinges, and all the tongue-tied lascivious 40 witnesses of great creatures' wantonness! What salvation can you expect?

PIETRO.
Wilt thou tell me?

MENDOZA.
Why, you may find it yourself; observe, observe.

PIETRO.
I ha' not the patience. Wilt thou deserve me? Tell, give it. 45

MENDOZA.
Take't! Why, Ferneze is the man, Ferneze. I'll prove't; this night you shall take him in your sheets. Will't serve?

PIETRO.
It will. My bosom's in some peace.
Till night—

MENDOZA. What?

PIETRO. Farewell.

MENDOZA. God! how weak a lord are you!
Why, do you think there is no more but so? 50

PIETRO.
Why?

MENDOZA. Nay, then will I presume to counsel you.
It should be thus: You with some guard upon the sudden
Break into the princess' chamber; I stay behind,
Without the door through which he needs must pass. 55
Ferneze flies—let him. To me he comes; he's kill'd
By me—observe, by me. You follow; I rail,
And seem to save the body. Duchess comes,
On whom (respecting her advanced birth

40. the] *Q; ye Q1–2.* 57. follow] *Q (corrected)*; fellow *Q (uncorrected)*.

---

40. *arras*] tapestry. 45. *deserve*] do service for.

And your fair nature) I know, nay, I do know, 60
No violence must be used. She comes; I storm,
I praise, excuse Ferneze, and still maintain
The duchess' honor; she for this loves me.
I honor you, shall know her soul, you mine;
Then naught shall she contrive in vengeance 65
(As women are most thoughtful in revenge)
Of her Ferneze, but you shall sooner know't
Than she can think't. Thus shall his death come sure;
Your duchess brain-caught, so your life secure.

PIETRO.
It is too well, my bosom and my heart! 70
When nothing helps, cut off the rotten part. *Exit.*

MENDOZA.
Who cannot feign friendship can ne'er produce the effects of hatred. Honest fool duke, subtle lascivious duchess, seely novice Ferneze—I do laugh at ye. My brain is in labor till it produce mischief; and I feel sudden throes, proofs sensible 75 the issue is at hand.
As bears shape young, so I'll form my device,
Which grown proves horrid: vengeance makes men wise.
[*Exit.*]

[I.viii] *Enter* Malevole *and* Passarello.

MALEVOLE.
Fool, most happily encounter'd. Canst sing, fool?

PASSARELLO.
Yes, I can sing, fool, if you'll bear the burden; and I can play upon instruments, scurvily, as gentlemen do. O, that I had been gelded! I should then have been a fat fool for a chamber, a squeaking fool for a tavern, and a private 5 fool for all the ladies.

78.1.] *Dodsley.*

I.viii.] *Neilson; not designated in Q; entire scene an addition in Q.*

---

69. *brain-caught*] betrayed by deception (B-P).
73. *seely*] innocent, foolish. 75. *sensible*] tangible.
[I.viii]
2. *bear the burden*] sing the refrain or the bass.

MALEVOLE.

You are in good case since you came to court, fool. What, guarded, guarded!

PASSARELLO.

Yes, faith, even as footmen and bawds wear velvet, not for an ornament of honor, but for a badge of drudgery; for, now the duke is discontented, I am fain to fool him asleep every night. 10

MALEVOLE.

What are his griefs?

PASSARELLO.

He hath sore eyes.

MALEVOLE.

I never observed so much. 15

PASSARELLO.

Horrible sore eyes; and so hath every cuckold, for the roots of the horns spring in the eyeballs; and that's the reason the horn of a cuckold is as tender as his eye, or as that growing in the woman's forehead twelve years since that could not endure to be touch'd. The duke hangs down his head like a columbine. 20

MALEVOLE.

Passarello, why do great men beg fools?

PASSARELLO.

As the Welshman stole rushes when there was nothing else to filch—only to keep begging in fashion.

MALEVOLE.

Pooh, thou givest no good reason; thou speakest like a fool. 25

---

7. *case*] garments.

8. *guarded*] fancily adorned, as with lace and braid.

19–20. *that growing . . . touch'd*] taken to refer to Margaret Griffith, wife of David Owen, of Llan Gaduain, in Montgomeryshire, whom a pamphlet of 1588 described as having "a crooked Horne of four ynches long" growing "in the midst of [her] forehead."

21. *columbine*] "The flower always points itself downwards" (Steevens); but cf.: "the horned nectaries suggested to an earlier age allusions of cuckoldry" (*OED*).

22. *beg fools*] seek the guardianship of idiots in order to enjoy the profits of their estates under the king's writ.

PASSARELLO.

Faith, I utter small fragments as your knight courts your city widow with jingling of his gilt spurs, advancing his bush-colored beard and taking tobacco. This is all the mirror of their knightly complements. Nay, I shall talk when my tongue is a-going once; 'tis like a citizen on horseback, evermore in a false gallop. 30

MALEVOLE.

And how doth Maquerelle fare nowadays?

PASSARELLO.

Faith, I was wont to salute her as our Englishwomen are at their first landing in Flushing: I would call her whore. But now that antiquity leaves her as an old piece of plastic t'work by, I only ask her how her rotten teeth fare every morning, and so leave her. She was the first that ever invented perfum'd smocks for the gentlewomen, and woolen shoes for fear of creaking for the visitant. She were an excellent lady but that her face peeleth like Muscovy glass. 35 40

MALEVOLE.

And how doth thy old lord that hath wit enough to be a flatterer and conscience enough to be a knave?

PASSARELLO.

O, excellent; he keeps beside me fifteen jesters to instruct him in the art of fooling, and utters their jests in private to the duke and duchess. He'll lie like to your Switzer or lawyer; he'll be of any side for most money. 45

MALEVOLE.

I am in haste; be brief.

PASSARELLO.

As your fiddler when he is paid. He'll thrive, I warrant you, while your young courtier stands like Good Friday in Lent;

27. jingling . . . advancing] Q (*corrected*); something of his guilt: some aduancing] Q (*uncorrected*).

28. bush-] Q (*corrected*); high Q (*uncorrected*).

29. *complements*] accomplishments.

34. *Flushing*] "At this time, *Flushing* was in the hands of the English as part of the security for money advanced by Queen Elizabeth to the Dutch. The governor and garrison were all Englishmen" (Reed).

40. *Muscovy glass*] talc.

45. *Switzer*] mercenary soldier.

men long to see it because more fatting days come after it; 50
else he's the leanest and pitifull'st actor in the whole
pageant. Adieu, Malevole.

MALEVOLE.

O world most vile, when thy loose vanities,
Taught by this fool, do make the fool seem wise!

PASSARELLO.

You'll know me again, Malevole. 55

MALEVOLE.

O, ay, by that velvet.

PASSARELLO.

Ay, as a pettifogger by his buckram bag. I am as common
in the court as an hostess's lips in the country; knights and
clowns and knaves and all share me; the court cannot
possibly be without me. Adieu, Malevole. [*Exeunt.*] 60

[II.i]

Enter Mendoza, *with a sconce, to observe* Ferneze's *entrance, who, whilst the act is playing, enter unbraced, two Pages before him with lights; is met by* Maquerelle *and conveyed in. The Pages are sent away.*

MENDOZA.

He's caught; the woodcock's head is i' th' noose.
Now treads Ferneze in dangerous path of lust,
Swearing his sense is merely deified.
The fool grasps clouds, and shall beget centaurs;
And now, in strength of panting, faint delight, 5
The goat bids heaven envy him. —Good goose,
I can afford thee nothing but the poor comfort of calamity,
pity.

53–54.] *Dyce makes this speech an aside.*
60. S.D.] *Dodsley.*
[II.i]
0.3. *Pages*] *Q, Q2; Dutches Pages Q1.*

57. *pettifogger*] lawyer of inferior status.
[II.i]
0.1. *sconce*] lantern.
0.2. *the act is playing*] referring to the entr'acte music between the acts at the private theaters.
0.2. *unbraced*] with garments unfastened (B-H-N).
1. *woodcock's*] dupe's. 3. *merely*] entirely.
4. *The fool . . . centaurs*] the fate of Ixion.

Lust's like the plummets hanging on clock-lines,
Will ne'er ha' done till all is quite undone.
Such is the course salt sallow lust doth run, 10
Which thou shalt try. I'll be reveng'd. Duke, thy suspect;
Duchess, thy disgrace; Ferneze, thy rivalship—
Shall have swift vengeance. Nothing so holy,
No band of nature so strong,
No law of friendship so sacred, 15
But I'll profane, burst, violate,
'Fore I'll endure disgrace, contempt, and poverty.
Shall I, whose very "Hum" struck all heads bare,
Whose face made silence, creaking of whose shoe
Forc'd the most private passages fly ope, 20
Scrape like a servile dog at some latch'd door?
Learn now to make a leg? and cry, "Beseech ye,
Pray ye, is such a lord within?"; be aw'd
At some odd usher's scoff'd formality?
First sear my brains! "*Unde cadis non quo, refert.*" 25
My heart cries, "Perish all!" How! how! What fate
Can once avoid revenge, that's desperate?
I'll to the duke. If all should ope—If? Tush!
Fortune still dotes on those who cannot blush. [*Exit.*]

[II.ii]

Enter Malevole *at one door;* Biancha, Emilia, *and* Maquerelle *at the other door.*

MALEVOLE.

Bless ye, cast o' ladies! —Ha, Dipsas! how dost thou, old coal?

9. quite undone] *Q;* quite is undone *Q1–2.*
25. sear] *Q1–2* (*seare*)*;* seate *Q.*
29. S.D.] *Dyce.*
[II.ii]
1. Dipsas!] *Q* (*corrected*)*;* dip-sawce *Q* (*uncorrected*).

10. *salt*] salacious. 22. *make a leg*] bow.
25. *Unde . . . refert*] "From whence you fall, not whither, is what matters" (adapted from Seneca's *Thyestes* 925–926).
[II.ii]
1. *cast*] pair (a term from falconry).
1. *Dipsas*] probably referring to the old enchantress in Lyly's *Endymion* whose "years are not so many as [her] vices." The name derives from a fabulous serpent whose bite afflicted its victim with unquenchable thirst.

MAQUERELLE.

Old coal!

MALEVOLE.

Ay, old coal; methinks thou liest like a brand under billets of green wood. He that will inflame a young wench's heart, 5 let him lay close to her an old coal that hath first been fired, a pand'ress, my half-burnt lint, who, though thou canst not flame thyself, yet art able to set a thousand virgins' tapers afire. —[*To* Biancha.] And how doth Janivere thy husband, my little periwinkle? Is he troubled with the cough of the 10 lungs still? Does he hawk a-nights still? He will not bite.

BIANCHA.

No, by my troth, I took him with his mouth empty of old teeth.

MALEVOLE.

And he took thee with thy belly full of young bones. Marry, he took his maim by the stroke of his enemy. 15

BIANCHA.

And I mine by the stroke of my friend.

MALEVOLE.

The close stock! O mortal wench! Lady, ha' ye now no restoratives for your decayed Jasons? Look ye, crabs' guts bak'd, distill'd ox-pith, the pulverized hairs of a lion's upper lip, jelly of cock-sparrows, he-monkeys' marrow, or 20 pouldre of fox-stones? —And whither are all you ambling now?

4. under billets] *Q;* under these billets *Q1–2.*
7. not] *Q* (*corrected*)*; not in Q* (*uncorrected*).
9. S.D.] *Q2; not in Q, Q1.*
9. doth] *Q;* do's *Q1–2.*
10. he] *Q;* a *Q1–2.*
21. pouldre] *Q* (*powlder*)*;* powder *Q1–2.*
21. are all you] *Q1–2*; are you *Q*.

4–5. *thou liest . . . wood*] Bullen aptly cites Overbury's *Characters*: "A maquerela, in plain English a bawd, is an old charcoal that hath been burnt herself, and therefore is able to kindle a whole green coppice."

9. *Janivere*] referring to Chaucer's story of the elderly January and his young wife May.

15. *maim*] injury.

17. *stock*] i.e., stoccado, thrust in fencing (with a *double entendre*).

18. *restoratives*] aphrodisiacs, such as the following.

21. *pouldre*] powder.

BIANCHA.

Why, to bed, to bed.

MALEVOLE.

Do your husbands lie with ye?

BIANCHA.

That were country fashion, i'faith. 25

MALEVOLE.

Ha' ye no foregoers about you? Come, whither in good deed, la now?

BIANCHA.

In good indeed, la now, to eat the most miraculously, admirably, astonishable-compos'd posset with three curds, without any drink. Will ye help me with a he-fox? —Here's 30 the duke.

The Ladies *go out.*

MALEVOLE (*to* Biancha).

Fried frogs are very good, and Frenchlike too!

[II.iii]

Enter Duke Pietro, Count Celso, Count Equato, Bilioso, Ferrardo, *and* Mendoza.

PIETRO.

The night grows deep and foul. What hour is't?

CELSO.

Upon the stroke of twelve.

MALEVOLE.

Save ye, duke!

PIETRO.

From thee! Begone, I do not love thee! Let me see thee no more; we are displeased. 5

MALEVOLE.

Why, God be with thee! Heaven hear my curse: May thy wife and thee live long together!

PIETRO.

Begone, sirrah!

23. Why,] *Q1–2; not in Q.*
28. S.P. BIANCHA] *Q; Maq. Q1–2.*
31.1.] *Q; Exeunt Ladies. Q1–2.*
32.] *addition Q.*
[II.iii]
6. be with] *Q;* buy *Q1–2.*

26. *foregoers*] gentlemen ushers.

MALEVOLE.

"When Arthur first in court began"—
Agamemnon—Menelaus—was ever any duke a *cornuto*? 10

PIETRO.

Begone hence!

MALEVOLE.

What religion wilt thou be of next?

MENDOZA.

Out with him!

MALEVOLE.

With most servile patience time will come
When wonder of thy error will strike dumb 15
Thy bezzl'd sense.—
Slave's i' favor, ay! Marry, shall he rise?
Good God! how subtle hell doth flatter vice,
Mounts him aloft and makes him seem to fly,
As fowl the tortoise mock'd, who to the sky 20
Th' ambitious shellfish rais'd! Th' end of all
Is only that from height he might dead fall.

BILIOSO.

Why, when? Out, ye rogue! Begone, ye rascal!

MALEVOLE.

"I shall now leave ye with all my best wishes."

BILIOSO.

Out, ye cur! 25

MALEVOLE.

"Only let's hold together a firm correspondence."

BILIOSO.

Out!

MALEVOLE.

"A mutual-friendly-reciprocal-perpetual kind of steady-unanimous-heartily-leagued—"

17.] slaues I fauour, I mary shall he, rise, *Qq*.

19. Mounts] *Q;* Mount *Q1–2*.

23–37.] *addition Q*.

---

9. "*When Arthur . . . began*"] the same ballad that Falstaff starts to sing in *II Henry IV*. Arthur, Agamemnon, Menelaus—all cuckolds.

16. *bezzl'd*] "muddled (with drinking)" (*OED*).

23. *Why, when?*] exclamation of impatience (Spencer). 24, 26, 28–29.] cf. I.iv.80–82.

BILIOSO.

Hence, ye gross-jaw'd, peasantly—out, go! 30

MALEVOLE.

Adieu, pigeon house; thou burr, that only stickest to nappy fortunes. The serpigo, the stranguary, an eternal uneffectual priapism seize thee!

BILIOSO.

Out, rogue!

MALEVOLE.

May'st thou be a notorious wittolly pander to thine own 35
wife, and yet get no office, but live to be the utmost misery of mankind, a beggarly cuckold! *Exit.*

PIETRO.

It shall be so.

MENDOZA.

It must be so, for where great states revenge
'Tis requisite the parts which piety 40
And loft respect forbears be closely dogg'd.
Lay one into his breast shall sleep with him,
Feed in the same dish, run in self-faction,
Who may discover any shape of danger;
For once disgrac'd, displayed in offense, 45
It makes man blushless, and man is (all confess)
More prone to vengeance than to gratefulness.
Favors are writ in dust, but stripes we feel
Depraved nature stamps in lasting steel.

PIETRO.

You shall be leagued with the duchess. 50

EQUATO.

The plot is very good.

MENDOZA.

You shall both kill and seem the corse to save.

40. which] *Spencer (and also MS. note in British Museum copy)*; with *Qq*.
41. loft] *Q, Q2;* soft *Q1.*
44. discover] *Q, Q2;* dissuer *Q1.*
45. displayed] *Q, Q2;* discouered *Q1.*

---

31. cf.] I.iv.83–85. 32. *nappy*] shaggy. 32. *serpigo*] ringworm.
32. *stranguary*] disease involving painful bladder disorder.
41. *loft*] proud. 52. *corse*] corpse.

FERRARDO.
A most fine brain-trick.

CELSO (*tacite*).
Of a most cunning knave.

PIETRO.
My lords, the heavy action we intend 55
Is death and shame, two of the ugliest shapes
That can confound a soul. Think, think of it.
I strike, but yet, like him that 'gainst stone walls
Directs his shafts, rebounds in his own face;
My lady's shame is mine, O God, 'tis mine! 60
Therefore, I do conjure all secrecy;
Let it be as very little as may be,
Pray ye, as may be.
Make frightless entrance, salute her with soft eyes,
Stain naught with blood. Only Ferneze dies, 65
But not before her brows. O Gentlemen,
God knows I love her! Nothing else, but this:
I am not well. If grief, that sucks veins dry,
Rivels the skin, casts ashes in men's faces,
Bedulls the eye, unstrengthens all the blood, 70
Chance to remove me to another world,
As sure I once must die, let him succeed:
I have no child; all that my youth begot
Hath been your loves, which shall inherit me;
Which as it ever shall, I do conjure it, 75
Mendoza may succeed; he's nobly born,
With me of much desert.

CELSO (*tacite*).
Much!

PIETRO.
Your silence answers, "Ay,"
I thank you. Come on now. O, that I might die 80

54. S.D.] *Q, Q2; not in Q1.*
65. Stain] *Q1;* Strain *Q, Q2.*
76. nobly] *Q1;* noble *Q, Q2.*
78. S.D.] *Q, Q2; not in Q1.*

54. S.D. *tacite*] silently (i.e., aside). 61. *conjure*] beseech.
65. *Stain . . . blood*] the reading of the third quarto could mean: "Urge [*strain*] nothing with passion [*blood*]."
69. *Rivels*] wrinkles. 74. *inherit*] be heir to (B-H-N).

Before her shame's display'd! Would I were forc'd
To burn my father's tomb, unhele his bones,
And dash them in the dirt, rather than this!
This both the living and the dead offends:
Sharp surgery where naught but death amends. 85

Exit with the others.

[II.iv] *Enter* Maquerelle, Emilia, *and* Biancha *with the posset.*

MAQUERELLE.
Even here it is, three curds in three regions individually distinct, most methodically according to art compos'd, without any drink.

BIANCHA.
Without any drink?

MAQUERELLE.
Upon my honor. Will you sit and eat? 5

EMILIA.
Good! The composure, the receipt, how is't?

MAQUERELLE.
'Tis a pretty pearl; by this pearl (how does't with me?) thus it is: seven and thirty yolks of Barbary hens' eggs; eighteen spoonfuls and a half of the juice of cock-sparrow bones; one ounce, three drams, four scruples, and one 10 quarter of the syrup of Ethiopian dates; sweeten'd with three-quarters of a pound of pure candied Indian eryngoes; strewed over with the powder of pearl of America, amber of Cataia, and lamb-stones of Muscovia.

BIANCHA.
Trust me, the ingredients are very cordial and, no question, 15 good and most powerful in restoration.

82. unhele] *Q* (*vnheale*); vnhill *Q1–2.*
[II.iv]
2. methodically] *Q1–2;* methodicall *Q.*
8. yolks] *Q1–2;* yelkes *Q.*
16. restoration] *Q, Q2;* operation *Q1.*

82. *unhele*] uncover.
[II.iv]
7. *how . . . me?*] "how does it become me?" (Neilson).
12. *eryngoes*] candied sea-holly root.
14. *Cataia*] Cathay (China).

MAQUERELLE.

I know not what you mean by restoration, but this it doth: it purifieth the blood, smootheth the skin, enliveneth the eye, strength'neth the veins, mundefieth the teeth, comforteth the stomach, fortifieth the back, and quick'neth the wit; that's all. 20

EMILIA.

By my troth, I have eaten but two spoonfuls, and methinks I could discourse most swiftly and wittily already.

MAQUERELLE.

Have you the art to seem honest?

BIANCHA.

I thank advice and practice. 25

MAQUERELLE.

Why, then, eat me of this posset, quicken your blood, and preserve your beauty. Do you know Doctor Plaster-face? By this curd, he is the most exquisite in forging of veins, spright'ning of eyes, dyeing of hair, sleeking of skins, blushing of cheeks, surfling of breasts, blanching and bleaching of teeth, that ever made an old lady gracious by torchlight; by this curd, la! 30

BIANCHA.

Well, we are resolved; what God has given us we'll cherish.

MAQUERELLE.

Cherish anything saving your husband; keep him not too high, lest he leap the pale. But, for your beauty, let it be your saint; bequeath two hours to it every morning in your closet. I ha' been young, and yet, in my conscience, I am not above five and twenty; but, believe me, preserve and use your beauty; for youth and beauty once gone, we are like beehives without honey, out-o'-fashion apparel that no man will wear; therefore, use me your beauty. 35 40

EMILIA.

Ay, but men say—

33. Well] *Q1–2;* We *Q*.

---

19. *mundefieth*] cleanseth. 24. *honest*] virtuous, chaste.
29. *spright'ning*] brightening.
30. *surfling*] painting or washing with a cosmetic (*OED*).
39. *use*] make profitable use of.

MAQUERELLE.
Men say! Let men say what they will. Life o' woman! they are ignorant of your wants. The more in years, the more in perfection they grow; if they lose youth and 45 beauty, they gain wisdom and discretion. But when our beauty fades, goodnight with us! There cannot be an uglier thing to see than an old woman, from which—O pruning, pinching, and painting!—deliver all sweet beauties! [*Music within.*] 50

BIANCHA.
Hark! music!

MAQUERELLE.
Peace, 'tis in the duchess' bedchamber. Good rest, most prosperously grac'd ladies.

EMILIA.
Good night, sentinel.

BIANCHA.
Night, dear Maquerelle. *Exeunt all but* Maquerelle. 55

MAQUERELLE.
May my posset's operation send you my wit and honesty; and me, your youth and beauty. The pleasing'st rest!

Exit Maquerelle.

[II.v] *A Song* [*within*].

Whilst the song is singing, enter Mendoza *with his sword drawn, standing ready to murder* Ferneze *as he flies from the* Duchess' *chamber.* [*Tumult within.*]

ALL [*within*].
Strike, strike!

AURELIA [*within*].
Save my Ferneze! O, save my Ferneze!

Enter Ferneze *in his shirt, and is received upon* Mendoza's *sword.*

44. your] *Q; our Q1–2.*
45. they grow] *Q;* the grow *Q1–2.*
50. S.D.] *Dyce.*
55. S.D.] *Q, Q2; Exeunt at seuerall dores. Q1.*
57.1.] *Q, Q2; Exit. Q1.*
[II.v]
0.1. *within*] *Dyce.*
0.3–4. *Tumult within*] *marginal S.D. in Q1–2; not in Q.*

ALL [*within*].
Follow, pursue!
AURELIA [*within*].
O, save Ferneze!
MENDOZA.
Pierce, pierce! (*Thrusts his rapier in* Ferneze.)
—Thou shallow fool, drop there! 5
He that attempts a princess' lawless love
Must have broad hands, close heart, with Argus' eyes,
And back of Hercules, or else he dies.

Enter Aurelia, Duke Pietro, Ferrardo, Bilioso, Celso, *and* Equato.

ALL.
Follow, follow!
[Mendoza *bestrides the wounded body of* Ferneze *and seems to save him.*]
MENDOZA.
Stand off, forbear, ye most uncivil lords! 10
PIETRO.
Strike!
MENDOZA.
Do not; tempt not a man resolved.
Would you, inhuman murderers, more than death?
AURELIA.
O poor Ferneze!
MENDOZA.
Alas, now all defense too late!
AURELIA. He's dead. 15
PIETRO.
I am sorry for our shame. —Go to your bed;
Weep not too much, but leave some tears to shed
When I am dead.
AURELIA.
What, weep for thee? My soul no tears shall find.
PIETRO.
Alas, alas, that women's souls are blind! 20
MENDOZA.
Betray such beauty!

5. S.D.] *after* dies (l. 8) *Q, Q2; not in Q1.*
9.1.] *Q1–2; not in Q.*

Murder such youth! Contemn civility!
He loves him not that rails not at him.

PIETRO.
Thou canst not move us: we have blood enough.—
And please you, lady, we have quite forgot 25
All your defects; if not, why, then—

AURELIA. Not.

PIETRO.
Not! The best of rest; good night.

Exit Pietro *with other* Courtiers.

AURELIA.
Despite go with thee!

MENDOZA.
Madam, you ha' done me foul disgrace.
You have wrong'd him much, loves you too much. 30
Go to, your soul knows you have.

AURELIA.
I think I have.

MENDOZA.
Do you but think so?

AURELIA.
Nay, sure I have; my eyes have witnessed thy love; thou
hast stood too firm for me. 35

MENDOZA.
Why, tell me, fair-cheek'd lady, who even in tears
Art powerfully beauteous, what unadvised passion
Struck ye into such a violent heat against me?
Speak, what mischief wrong'd us? What devil injur'd us?
Speak. 40

AURELIA.
That thing ne'er worthy of the name of man, Ferneze.
Ferneze swore thou lov'st Emilia;
Which to advance, with most reproachful breath
Thou both didst blemish and denounce my love.

MENDOZA.
Ignoble villain, did I for this bestride 45

---

30. *loves*] i.e., who loves.

Thy wounded limbs? For this, rank opposite
Even to my sovereign? For this, O God! for this
Sunk all my hopes, and with my hopes my life?
Ripp'd bare my throat unto the hangman's ax?—
Thou most dishonor'd trunk!—Emilia! 50
By life, I know her not—Emilia!—
Did you believe him?

AURELIA. Pardon me, I did.

MENDOZA.
Did you? And thereupon you graced him?

AURELIA.
I did.

MENDOZA.
Took him to favor, nay, even clasp'd with him? 55

AURELIA.
Alas, I did!

MENDOZA. This night?

AURELIA. This night.

MENDOZA.
And in your lustful twines the duke took you?

AURELIA.
A most sad truth.

MENDOZA.
O God, O God! How we dull honest souls,
Heavy-brain'd men, are swallowed in the bogs 60
Of a deceitful ground, whilst nimble bloods,
Light-jointed spirits, pent, cut good men's throats
And scape! Alas, I am too honest for this age,
Too full of phlegm and heavy steadiness;
Stood still whilst this slave cast a noose about me; 65
Nay, then, to stand in honor of him and her,

46–47. For . . . sovereign?] *Q1–2; not in Q*. 62. pent] *Q1–2;* spent *Q*.

---

46. *rank opposite*] oppose. 55. *clasp'd*] embraced.
62. *pent*] confined within narrow limits.
64. *Too full of phlegm*] i.e., out of "humor" with his age.

Who had even slic'd my heart.

AURELIA. Come, I did err,

And am most sorry I did err.

MENDOZA.

Why, we are both but dead; the duke hates us.
And those whom princes do once groundly hate, 70
Let them provide to die, as sure as fate.
Prevention is the heart of policy.

AURELIA.

Shall we murder him?

MENDOZA.

Instantly.

AURELIA.

Instantly, before he casts a plot, 75
Or further blaze my honor's much-known blot,
Let's murder him!

MENDOZA.

I would do much for you; will ye marry me?

AURELIA.

I'll make thee duke. We are of Medicis;
Florence our friend; in court my faction 80
Not meanly strengthful; the duke then dead;
We well prepar'd for change; the multitude
Irresolutely reeling; we in force;
Our party seconded; the kingdom maz'd;
No doubt of swift success—all shall be grac'd. 85

MENDOZA.

You do confirm me; we are resolute.
Tomorrow look for change; rest confident.
'Tis now about the immodest waist of night;
The mother of moist dew with pallid light
Spreads gloomy shades about the numbed earth. 90

---

70. *groundly*] thoroughly. 71. *provide*] prepare.
72. *Prevention*] caution, anticipation. 76. *blaze*] blazon (proclaim).
79. *Medicis*] "The Medici family was popularly associated in the Elizabethan mind with the idea of Machiavellian craft and unscrupulousness" (Wood).
81. *Not meanly*] not moderately, i.e., very.
84. *maz'd*] confused. 88. *waist*] middle.

Sleep, sleep, whilst we contrive our mischief's birth.
This man I'll get inhum'd. Farewell; to bed.
Ay, kiss thy pillow; dream the duke is dead.
So, so, good night. *Exit* Aurelia.
—How fortune dotes on impudence!
I am in private the adopted son of yon good prince. 95
I must be duke. Why, if I must, I must!
Most seely lord, name me! O Heaven!
I see God made honest fools to maintain crafty knaves.
The duchess is wholly mine too; must kill her husband
To quit her shame. Much! Then marry her! Ay! 100
O, I grow proud in prosperous treachery!
As wrestlers clip, so I'll embrace you all,
Not to support, but to procure your fall.

Enter Malevole.

MALEVOLE.
God arrest thee!

MENDOZA.
At whose suit? 105

MALEVOLE.
At the devil's. Ah, you treacherous damnable monster! How dost? How dost, thou treacherous rogue? Ah, ye rascal! I am banish'd the court, sirrah.

MENDOZA.
Prithee, let's be acquainted; I do love thee, faith.

MALEVOLE.
At your service, by the Lord, la! Shall's go to supper? 110 Let's be once drunk together, and so unite a most virtuously strengthened friendship. Shall's, Huguenot? Shall's?

MENDOZA.
Wilt fall upon my chamber tomorrow morn?

MALEVOLE.
As a raven to a dunghill. They say there's one dead here, prick'd for the pride of the flesh. 115

93. thy] *Q1–2*; the *Q*. 97. seely] *Q*; silly *Q1–2*.

---

92. *inhum'd*] buried. 97. *seely*] cf. I.vii.73.
112. *Huguenot*] French Protestants; used here in the sense of "hypocrite" or "traitor."

MENDOZA.

Ferneze. There he is; prithee, bury him.

MALEVOLE.

O, most willingly; I mean to turn pure Rochelle churchman, I.

MENDOZA.

Thou churchman! Why, why?

MALEVOLE.

Because I'll live lazily, rail upon authority, deny kings' supremacy in things indifferent, and be a pope in mine own parish. 120

MENDOZA.

Wherefore dost thou think churches were made?

MALEVOLE.

To scour plowshares; I have seen oxen plow up altars; "*et nunc seges ubi Sion fuit.*" 125

MENDOZA.

Strange!

MALEVOLE.

Nay, monstrous! I ha' seen a sumptuous steeple turn'd to a stinking privy; more beastly, the sacred'st place made a dogs' kennel; nay, most inhuman, the stoned coffins of long-dead Christians burst up and made hogs' troughs: "*hic finis Priami.*" Shall I ha' some sack and cheese at thy chamber? Good night, good mischievous incarnate devil; good night, Mendoza. Ah, you inhuman villain, good night! Night, fub. 130

MENDOZA.

Good night; tomorrow morn. *Exit* Mendoza.

MALEVOLE.

Ay, I will come, friendly damnation, I will come. I do descry cross-points; honesty and courtship straddle as far asunder as a true Frenchman's legs. 135

124. have] *Q;* ha *Q1–2.*

---

117. *Rochelle*] where the Huguenots found refuge from persecution.

124–125. *et nunc . . . fuit*] "And now corn-fields exist where Sion was" (adapted from Ovid's *Heroical Epistles* i. 53).

130–131. *hic finis Priami*] incorrect version of Virgil's *haec finis Priami fatorum* ("Such was Priam's ill fate," *Aeneid* II. 554).

133. *fub*] cheat.

136. *cross-points*] steps in dancing; here, tricks.

136. *courtship*] courtiership (Spencer).

FERNEZE.
O!

MALEVOLE.
Proclamations! More proclamations!

FERNEZE.
O! a surgeon! 140

MALEVOLE.
Hark! lust cries for a surgeon. —What news from Limbo?
How doth the grand cuckold, Lucifer?

FERNEZE.
O, help, help! Conceal and save me.

Ferneze *stirs, and* Malevole *helps him up and conveys him away.*

MALEVOLE.
Thy shame more than thy wounds do grieve me far;
Thy wounds but leave upon thy flesh some scar, 145
But fame ne'er heals, still rankles worse and worse;
Such is of uncontrolled lust the curse.
Think what it is in lawless sheets to lie;
But, O, Ferneze, what in lust to die!
Then thou that shame respects, O, fly converse 150
With women's eyes and lisping wantonness!
Stick candles 'gainst a virgin wall's white back:
If they not burn, yet at the least they'll black.
Come, I'll convey thee to a private port
Where thou shalt live, O happy man, from court. 155
The beauty of the day begins to rise,
From whose bright form night's heavy shadow flies.
Now 'gins close plots to work; the scene grows full,
And craves his eyes who hath a solid skull. *Exeunt.*

[III.i]

Enter Pietro the Duke, Mendoza, Count Equato, *and* Bilioso.

PIETRO.
'Tis grown to youth of day; how shall we waste this light?
My heart's more heavy than a tyrant's crown.
Shall we go hunt? Prepare for field. *Exit* Equato.

142. doth] *Q;* does *Q1–2.*

146. *fame*] infamy.
158. *'gins*] begins. 159. *solid skull*] sound head (B-H-N).

MENDOZA.

Would ye could be merry!

PIETRO.

Would God I could! Mendoza, bid 'em haste. 5

Exit Mendoza.

I would fain shift place; O vain relief!
Sad souls may well change place, but not change grief.
As deer, being struck, fly thorough many soils,
Yet still the shaft sticks fast, so—

BILIOSO.

A good old simile, my honest lord. 10

PIETRO.

I am not much unlike to some sick man
That long desired hurtful drink; at last
Swills in and drinks his last, ending at once
Both life and thirst. O, would I ne'er had known
My own dishonor! Good God, that men should 15
Desire to search out that which, being found, kills all
Their joy of life! To taste the tree of knowledge,
And then be driven from out paradise!
Canst give me some comfort?

BILIOSO.

My lord, I have some books which have been dedicated 20
to my honor, and I ne'er read 'em; and yet they had very
fine names: *Physic for Fortune*, *Lozenges of Sanctified Sincerity*;
very pretty works of curates, scriveners, and schoolmasters.
Marry, I remember one Seneca, Lucius Annæus Seneca—

PIETRO.

Out upon him! He writ of temperance and fortitude, yet 25
lived like a voluptuous epicure and died like an effeminate
coward.

10. S.P. BILIOSO.] *Q; Mend. Q2; line given to Pietro in Q1.*

---

8. *soils*] pools or stretches of water "used as a refuge by a hunted deer or other animal" (*OED*).

22. *Physic for Fortune*] Reed suggests perhaps the book *Physick against fortune*, translated from the Latin of Petrarch by Thomas Twyne, and published in 1579. But both titles mentioned probably are meant to suggest Puritan pamphlets.

24. *Seneca*] "The Philosopher" (*c.* 4 B.C.—A.D. 65), noted for his Stoic "Dialogues," treatises, and tragedies.

Haste thee to Florence.
Here, take our letters; see 'em seal'd; away!
Report in private to the honor'd duke 30
His daughter's forc'd disgrace; tell him at length
We know too much; due compliments advance.
There's naught that's safe and sweet but ignorance.

Exit Duke.

Enter Biancha.

BILIOSO.
Madam, I am going ambassador for Florence; 'twill be great charges to me. 35

BIANCHA.
No matter, my lord, you have the lease of two manors come out next Christmas; you may lay your tenants on the greater rack for it; and, when you come home again, I'll teach you how you shall get two hundred pounds a year by your teeth. 40

BILIOSO.
How, madam?

BIANCHA.
Cut off so much from housekeeping; that which is saved by the teeth, you know, is got by the teeth.

BILIOSO.
'Fore God, and so I may; I am in wondrous credit, lady.

BIANCHA.
See the use of flattery; I did ever counsel you to flatter 45 greatness, and you have profited well. Any man that will do so shall be sure to be like your Scotch barnacle, now a

28–31.] *Dyce; as prose Qq.*
32. compliments] *Q;* complaints *Q1–2.*
33.2–146.] *addition Q.*
33.2.] *Enter Bilioso and Bianca Q.*

36–37. *come out*] "run out," expire.

37–38. *may lay . . . greater rack*] "strain your tenants to the utmost for greater rent."

47. *Scotch barnacle*] Wood cites Gerard's *Herball*, Chap. 188 (1597): "There are found in the North parts of Scotland and the Islands adjacent, called Orchades, certaine trees [Goose trees, Barnacle trees, or the trees bearing Geese] whereon do grow certaine shells of a white colour tending to russet, wherein are contained little living creatures: which shells in time of maturity doe open, and out of them grow those little living things, which falling into the water do become fowles, which we call Barnacles."

block, instantly a worm, and presently a great goose: this it is to rot and putrefy in the bosom of greatness.

BILIOSO.

Thou art ever my politician. O, how happy is that old lord that hath a politician to his young lady! I'll have fifty gentlemen shall attend upon me; marry, the most of them shall be farmers' sons because they shall bear their own charges, and they shall go appareled thus—in sea-water green suits, ash-color cloaks, watchet stockings, and popinjay-green feathers. Will not the colors do excellent? 50 55

BIANCHA.

Out upon't! They'll look like citizens riding to their friends at Whitsuntide, their apparel just so many several parishes.

BILIOSO.

I'll have it so; and Passarello, my fool, shall go along with me; marry, he shall be in velvet. 60

BIANCHA.

A fool in velvet?

BILIOSO.

Ay, 'tis common for your fool to wear satin; I'll have mine in velvet.

BIANCHA.

What will you wear, then, my lord?

BILIOSO.

Velvet, too; marry, it shall be embroidered because I'll differ from the fool somewhat. I am horribly troubled with the gout; nothing grieves me but that my doctor hath forbidden me wine, and you know your ambassador must drink. Didst thou ask thy doctor what was good for the gout? 65 70

BIANCHA.

Yes; he said ease, wine, and women were good for it.

BILIOSO.

Nay, thou hast such a wit! What was good to cure it, said he?

---

48. *block*] stump of a tree.
55. *watchet*] pale blue.
58. *their . . . parishes*] i.e., mismatched (B-H-N).

BIANCHA.

Why, the rack. All your empirics could never do the like cure upon the gout the rack did in England, or your Scotch boot. The French harlequin will instruct you. 75

BILIOSO.

Surely, I do wonder how thou, having for the most part of thy lifetime been a country body, shouldest have so good a wit.

BIANCHA.

Who, I? Why, I have been a courtier thrice two months. 80

BILIOSO.

So have I this twenty year, and yet there was a gentleman usher call'd me coxcomb t'other day, and to my face too. Was't not a backbiting rascal? I would I were better travel'd, that I might have been better acquainted with the fashions of several countrymen; but my secretary, I think, he hath sufficiently instructed me. 85

BIANCHA.

How, my lord?

BILIOSO.

"Marry, my good lord," quoth he, "your lordship shall ever find amongst a hundred Frenchmen forty hot-shots; amongst a hundred Spaniards, threescore braggarts; amongst a hundred Dutchmen, fourscore drunkards; amongst a hundred Englishmen, fourscore and ten madmen; and amongst an hundred Welshmen"— 90

BIANCHA.

What, my lord?

BILIOSO.

"Fourscore and nineteen gentlemen." 95

---

74. *empirics*] medical practitioners who rely "solely on observation and experiment"; often in the sense of "a quack" (*OED*).

75–76. *Scotch boot*] tightly fitted iron boots, into which wedges were driven between them and the leg of the prisoner.

76. *The French . . . you*] "Any empiric's zany will tell you" (Spencer).

82. *coxcomb*] conceited fool.

85. *several countrymen*] men of different countries (B-P).

89. *hot-shots*] reckless hotheads.

95. *Fourscore . . . gentlemen*] alluding to the pride that the Welsh proverbially have in their nation.

BIANCHA.

But, since you go about a sad embassy, I would have you go in black, my lord.

BILIOSO.

Why, dost think I cannot mourn unless I wear my hat in cypress, like an alderman's heir? That's vile, very old, in faith. 100

BIANCHA.

I'll learn of you shortly. O, we should have a fine gallant of you, should not I instruct you! How will you bear yourself when you come into the Duke of Florence' court?

BILIOSO.

Proud enough, and 'twill do well enough. As I walk up and down the chamber, I'll spit frowns about me, have a strong 105 perfume in my jerkin, let my beard grow to make me look terrible, salute no man beneath the fourth button; and 'twill do excellent.

BIANCHA.

But there is a very beautiful lady there; how will you entertain her? 110

BILIOSO.

I'll tell you that when the lady hath entertain'd me. But to satisfy thee, here comes the fool.

Enter Passarello.

Fool, thou shalt stand for the fair lady.

PASSARELLO.

Your fool will stand for your lady most willingly and most uprightly. 115

BILIOSO.

I'll salute her in Latin.

PASSARELLO.

O, your fool can understand no Latin.

BILIOSO.

Ay, but your lady can.

112.1.] *after* lady (*l. 113*) *Q*.

---

99. *cypress*] a light, transparent crape-like material.
114–115. *Your . . . uprightly*] with *double entendre*.

PASSARELLO.

Why, then, if your lady take down your fool, your fool will stand no longer for your lady. 120

BILIOSO.

A pestilent fool! 'Fore God, I think the world be turn'd upside down too.

PASSARELLO.

O, no, sir; for then your lady and all the ladies in the palace should go with their heels upward, and that were a strange sight, you know. 125

BILIOSO.

There be many will repine at my preferment.

PASSARELLO.

O, ay, like the envy of an elder sister that hath her younger made a lady before her.

BILIOSO.

The duke is wondrous discontented.

PASSARELLO.

Ay, and more melancholic than a usurer having all his 130 money out at the death of a prince.

BILIOSO.

Didst thou see Madam Floria today?

PASSARELLO.

Yes, I found her repairing her face today. The red upon the white showed as if her cheeks should have been served in for two dishes of barberries in stewed broth, and the flesh 135 to them a woodcock.

BILIOSO.

A bitter fowl! Come, madam, this night thou shalt enjoy me freely, and tomorrow for Florence. [*Exeunt* Bilioso *and* Biancha.]

PASSARELLO

What a natural fool is he that would be a pair of bodies to a woman's petticoat, to be truss'd and pointed to them! Well, 140 I'll dog my lord; and the word is proper, for, when I fawn upon him, he feeds me; when I snap him by the fingers, he

---

126. *preferment*] advancement or promotion.
137. *fowl*] pun on *fool* perhaps.
139. *bodies*] bodice, stays.
140. *truss'd and pointed*] tied and laced (the hose to the doublet).

spits in my mouth. If a dog's death were not strangling, I had rather be one than a serving-man; for the corruption of coin is either the generation of a usurer or a lousy 145
beggar. *Exit.*

[III.ii]

Enter Malevole *in some frieze gown, whilst* Bilioso *reads his patent.*

MALEVOLE.

I cannot sleep; my eyes' ill-neighboring lids
Will hold no fellowship. O thou pale, sober night,
Thou that in sluggish fumes all sense dost steep;
Thou that gives all the world full leave to play,
Unbend'st the feebled veins of sweaty labor! 5
The galley-slave, that all the toilsome day
Tugs at his oar against the stubborn wave,
Straining his rugged veins, snores fast;
The stooping scythe-man, that doth barb the field,
Thou makest wink sure. In night all creatures sleep; 10
Only the malcontent, that 'gainst his fate
Repines and quarrels, alas, he's goodman tell-clock!
His sallow jawbones sink with wasting moan;
Whilst others' beds are down, his pillow's stone.

BILIOSO.

Malevole! 15

MALEVOLE (*to* Bilioso).

Elder of Israel, thou honest defect of wicked nature and obstinate ignorance, when did thy wife let thee lie with her?

BILIOSO.

I am going ambassador to Florence.

MALEVOLE.

Ambassador! Now, for thy country's honor, prithee, do 20

146. S.D.] *after* woodcock (*l. 136*) Q.

[III.ii]
16. S.D.] *Q, Q2; not in Q1.*

0.1. *frieze*] coarse woolen cloth.
0.1. *whilst . . . patent*] in the unaugmented editions Bilioso has not left the stage.
0.1. *patent*] letter of appointment as ambassador.
9. *barb*] mow. 10. *wink*] sleep.
12. *tell-clock*] "teller" (i.e., counter) of the clock.

not put up mutton and porridge in thy cloak bag. Thy young lady wife goes to Florence with thee too, does she not?

BILIOSO.

No, I leave her at the palace.

MALEVOLE.

At the palace! Now, discretion shield, man! For God's love, let's ha' no more cuckolds! Hymen begins to put off his 25
saffron robe; keep thy wife i' the state of grace. Heart o' truth, I would sooner leave my lady singled in a bordello than in the Genoa palace.
Sin, there appearing in her sluttish shape,
Would soon grow loathsome, even to blushes' sense; 30
Surfeit would cloak intemperate appetite,
Make the soul scent the rotten breath of lust.
When in an Italian lascivious palace, a lady guardianless,
Left to the push of all allurement,
The strongest incitements to immodesty, 35
To have her bound, incens'd with wanton sweets,
Her veins fill'd high with heating delicates,
Soft rest, sweet music, amorous masquerers,
Lascivious banquets, sin itself gilt o'er,
Strong fantasy tricking up strange delights, 40
Presenting it dressed pleasingly to sense,
Sense leading it unto the soul, confirm'd
With potent example, impudent custom,
Entic'd by that great bawd, Opportunity—
Thus being prepar'd, clap to her easy ear 45
Youth in good clothes, well-shap'd, rich,
Fair-spoken, promising-noble, ardent, blood-full,
Witty, flattering—Ulysses absent,
O Ithaca, can chastest Penelope hold out?

BILIOSO.

Mass, I'll think on't. Farewell. 50

38–49.] *Dodsley; as prose Qq.*
49. Ithaca, can chastest] *Q1–2;* *Ithacan,* chastest *Q.*

24. *shield*] forbid.
25–26. *Hymen . . . saffron robe*] "Hymen was usually represented in masques with a saffron robe" (Bullen).
27. *singled*] alone. 27. *bordello*] brothel.
29. *there*] in the bordello.

MALEVOLE.

Farewell. Take thy wife with thee. Farewell. *Exit* Bilioso.
To Florence, um? It may prove good, it may!
And we may once unmask our brows.

[III.iii] *Enter* Count Celso.

CELSO.

My honor'd lord—

MALEVOLE.

Celso, peace! How is't? Speak low. Pale fears suspect that
hedges, walls, and trees have ears. Speak; how runs all?

CELSO.

I' faith, my lord, that beast with many heads,
The staggering multitude, recoils apace. 5
Though thorough great men's envy, most men's malice,
Their much intemperate heat hath banish'd you,
Yet now they find envy and malice ne'er
Produce faint reformation.
The duke, the too soft duke, lies as a block, 10
For which two tugging factions seem to saw;
But still the iron through the ribs they draw.

MALEVOLE.

I tell thee, Celso, I have ever found
Thy breast most far from shifting cowardice
And fearful baseness; therefore, I'll tell thee, Celso, 15
I find the wind begins to come about;
I'll shift my suit of fortune.
I know the Florentine, whose only force,
By marrying his proud daughter to this prince,
Both banish'd me and made this weak lord duke, 20
Will now forsake them all; be sure he will.
I'll lie in ambush for conveniency,
Upon their severance to confirm myself.

CELSO.

Is Ferneze interred?

51. S.D.] *after l. 50 Q*.

[III.iii]
8. find] *Q*, *Q2*; faind *Q1*.

18. *only force*] power alone.
23. *confirm myself*] strengthen my position (B-P).

MALEVOLE.
Of that at leisure; he lives. 25

CELSO.
But how stands Mendoza? How is't with him?

MALEVOLE.
Faith, like a pair of snuffers, snibs filth in other men and retains it in itself.

CELSO.
He does fly from public notice, methinks, as a hare does from hounds; the feet whereon he flies betrays him. 30

MALEVOLE.
I can track him, Celso.
O, my disguise fools him most powerfully!
For that I seem a desperate malcontent,
He fain would clasp with me; he is the true slave
That will put on the most affected grace 35
For some vile second cause.

Enter Mendoza.

CELSO. He's here.

MALEVOLE. Give place.— *Exit* Celso.
Illo, ho, ho, ho! art there, old truepenny? Where hast thou spent thyself this morning? I see flattery in thine eyes and damnation in thy soul. Ha, thou huge rascal!

MENDOZA.
Thou art very merry. 40

MALEVOLE.
As a scholar, *futuens gratis*. How doth the devil go with thee now?

MENDOZA.
Malevole, thou art an arrant knave.

28. itself] *Q;* himself *Q1–2.*
36. S.D. *Exit* Celso] *after* truepenny (*l. 37*) *Qq.*
39. thou] *Q;* ye *Q1–2.*
41. doth] *Q;* doz *Q1–2.*

---

27. *snibs*] rebukes. 36. *second*] lesser.
37. *Illo, ho, ho, ho!*] the cry of the falconer, luring the hawk.
41. *futuens gratis*] loving without having to pay.

MALEVOLE.

Who, I? I have been a sergeant, man.

MENDOZA.

Thou art very poor. 45

MALEVOLE.

As Job, an alchemist, or a poet.

MENDOZA.

The duke hates thee.

MALEVOLE.

As Irishmen do bum-cracks.

MENDOZA.

Thou hast lost his amity.

MALEVOLE.

As pleasing as maids lose their virginity. 50

MENDOZA.

Would thou wert of a lusty spirit! Would thou wert noble!

MALEVOLE.

Why, sure my blood gives me I am noble, sure I am of noble kind; for I find myself possessed with all their qualities: love dogs, dice, and drabs; scorn wit in stuff-clothes; have beat my shoemaker, knock'd my seamstress, 55 cuckold' my 'pothecary, and undone my tailor. Noble! Why not? Since the stoic said, "*Neminem servum non ex regibus, neminem regem non ex servis esse oriundum*," only busy Fortune touses, and the provident Chances blends them together. I'll give you a simile. Did you e're see a well with 60 two buckets, whilst one comes up full to be emptied, another goes down empty to be filled? Such is the state of all humanity. Why, look you, I may be the son of some duke; for, believe me, intemperate lascivious bastardy

---

44. *sergeant*] sheriff's officer.

48. *As . . . bum-cracks*] Wood quotes Nashe's *Pierce Penilesse*: "The Irishman will drawe his dagger, and bee ready to kill and slay, if one breake winde in his company."

52. *gives*] informs.

54. *stuff-*] coarse material.

57–58. *Neminem . . . oriundum*] "There is no slave who does not descend from kings, no king who does not take his origin from slaves"—Seneca, Epistle XLIV, quoting Plato.

59. *touses*] "pulls roughly about" (*OED*).

makes nobility doubtful. I have a lusty, daring heart, 65
Mendoza.

MENDOZA.
Let's grasp; I do like thee infinitely. Wilt enact one thing for me?

MALEVOLE.
Shall I get by it? ([Mendoza] *gives him his purse.*) Command me; I am thy slave, beyond death and hell. 70

MENDOZA.
Murder the duke.

MALEVOLE.
My heart's wish, my soul's desire, my fantasy's dream, my blood's longing, the only height of my hopes! How, O God, how? O, how my united spirits throng together! So strengthen my resolve! 75

MENDOZA.
The duke is now a-hunting.

MALEVOLE.
Excellent, admirable, as the devil would have it! Lend me, lend me rapier, pistol, crossbow; so, so, I'll do it.

MENDOZA.
Then we agree.

MALEVOLE.
As Lent and fishmongers. Come, a-cap-a-pe, how? 80
Inform.

MENDOZA.
Know that this weak-brain'd duke, who only stands
On Florence' stilts, hath out of witless zeal
Made me his heir and secretly confirm'd
The wreath to me after his life's full point. 85

MALEVOLE.
Upon what merit?

MENDOZA. Merit! By heaven, I horn him.
Only Ferneze's death gave me state's life.
Tut, we are politic; he must not live now.

69. S.D. Mendoza] *Dyce.* 82–89.] *Dodsley; as prose Qq.*

---

67. *grasp*] embrace.
80. *a-cap-a-pe*] from head to foot. 85. *point*] "period," end.

MALEVOLE.

No reason, marry. But how must he die now?

MENDOZA.

My utmost project is to murder the duke, that I might have his state, because he makes me his heir; to banish the duchess, that I might be rid of a cunning Lacedæmonian, because I know Florence will forsake her; and then to marry Maria, the banished Duke Altofront's wife, that her friends might strengthen me and my faction; this is all, la. 90 95

MALEVOLE.

Do you love Maria?

MENDOZA.

Faith, no great affection, but as wise men do love great women, to ennoble their blood and augment their revenue. To accomplish this now, thus now: The Duke is in the forest, next the sea; single him, kill him, hurl him in the main, and proclaim thou sawest wolves eat him. 100

MALEVOLE.

Um! Not so good. Methinks, when he is slain,
To get some hypocrite, some dangerous wretch,
That's muffled o'er with feigned holiness, 105
To swear he heard the duke on some steep cliff
Lament his wife's dishonor, and, in an agony
Of his heart's torture, hurled his groaning sides
Into the swoll'n sea. This circumstance,
Well made, sounds probable; and hereupon 110
The duchess—

MENDOZA. May well be banished.

O unpeerable invention! Rare!
Thou god of policy, it honeys me!

MALEVOLE.

Then fear not for the wife of Altofront;

103–122.] *Dodsley; as prose Qq.*

92. *Lacedæmonian*] slang for strumpet (B-P).
109. *circumstance*] detailed narration (*OED*).
112. *unpeerable*] peerless, unrivaled.

I'll close to her. 115

MENDOZA.

Thou shalt, thou shalt. Our excellency is pleas'd.
Why wert not thou an emperor? When we
Are duke, I'll make thee some great man, sure.

MALEVOLE.

Nay, make me some rich knave, and I'll make myself
Some great man.

MENDOZA. In thee be all my spirit; 120
Retain ten souls; unite thy virtual powers.
Resolve; ha, remember greatness! Heart, farewell.

Enter Celso.

The fate of all my hopes in thee doth dwell. [*Exit.*]

MALEVOLE.

Celso, didst hear? O heaven, didst hear
Such devilish mischief? Sufferest thou the world 125
Carouse damnation even with greedy swallow,
And still dost wink, still does thy vengeance slumber?
If now thy brows are clear, when will they thunder?

[*Exeunt.*]

[III.iv] *Enter* Pietro, Ferrardo, Prepasso, *and three* Pages.

FERRARDO.

The dogs are at fault. *Cornets like horns.*

PIETRO.

Would God nothing but the dogs were at it! Let the deer
pursue safely, the dogs follow the game, and do you follow
the dogs. As for me, 'tis unfit one beast should hunt another.
I ha' one chaseth me; and't please you, I would be rid of you 5
a little.

123. S.D.] *Dodsley.*
128.1. *Exeunt*] *Dodsley; Exit. Qq.*

[III.iv]
5. and't] *Q;* and *Q1–2.*

115. *close to*] reach an agreement with.
121. *virtual*] "morally virtuous" (*OED*).

[III.iv]
3. *pursue*] run on (Spencer).
4. *one beast*] i.e., the duke himself as a horned cuckold.

FERRADO.

Would your grief would as soon leave you as we to quietness.

PIETRO.

I thank you.— *Exeunt* [Ferrardo *and* Prepasso].

Boy, what dost thou dream of now?

I PAGE.

Of a dry summer, my lord; for here's a hot world towards. 10

But, my lord, I had a strange dream last night.

PIETRO.

What strange dream?

I PAGE.

Why, methought I pleased you with singing, and then I dreamt you gave me that short sword.

PIETRO.

Prettily begg'd; hold thee, I'll prove thy dream true—tak't. 15

I PAGE.

My duty. But still I dreamt on, my lord; and methought, and't shall please your excellency, you would needs out of your royal bounty give me that jewel in your hat.

PIETRO.

O, thou didst but dream, boy; do not believe it. Dreams prove not always true; they may hold in a short sword, but 20 not in a jewel. But now, sir, you dreamt you had pleased me with singing; make that true, as I have made the other.

I PAGE.

Faith, my lord, I did but dream; and dreams, you say, prove not always true: they may hold in a good sword, but not in a good song. The truth is, I ha' lost my voice. 25

PIETRO.

Lost thy voice! How?

I PAGE.

With dreaming, faith. But here's a couple of sirenical rascals shall enchant ye. What shall they sing, my good lord?

PIETRO.

Sing of the nature of women, and then the song shall be

7. as soon leave you as we] *Q;* as soone as wee, leave you *Q1–2.*
8. S.D. Ferrardo *and* Prepasso] *Dodsley.*
10. S.P. I] *Dyce.*
22. have] *Q;* ha *Q1–2.*

10. *towards*] approaching. 27. *sirenical*] melodious.

surely full of variety, old crotchets, and most sweet closes; 30
it shall be humorous, grave, fantastic, amorous, melancholy,
sprightly, one in all, and all in one.

I PAGE.
All in one!

PIETRO.
By'r Lady, too many. Sing! My speech grows culpable of
unthrifty idleness. Sing! 35

Song [*By* 2 *and* 3 Pages].

[III.v] *Enter* Malevole, *with crossbow and pistol.*

PIETRO.
Ah, so, so, sing. I am heavy. Walk off; I shall talk in my
sleep; walk off. *Exeunt* Pages.

MALEVOLE.
Brief, brief! who? The duke! Good heaven, that fools should
stumble upon greatness! —Do not sleep, duke; give ye good
morrow. You must be brief, duke; I am feed to murder thee. 5
Start not! Mendoza, Mendoza hired me; here's his gold,
his pistol, crossbow, and sword—'tis all as firm as earth.
O fool, fool, chok'd with the common maze of easy idiots!
Credulity, make him thine heir! What, thy sworn murderer!

PIETRO.
O, can it be? 10

MALEVOLE.
Can!

PIETRO.
Discovered he not Ferneze?

MALEVOLE.
Yes, but why? but why? For love to thee? Much, much!
To be revenged upon his rival, who had thrust his jaws

35.1. *By* 2 *and* 3 Pages] *Dyce.*
[III.v]
1. S.P. PIETRO.] *Neilson; not in Qq.*
5. You] *Q; not in Q1–2.*
7. and] *Q; not in Q1–2.*

30. *crotchets*] quarter notes, with pun on meaning of whimsical fancies.
30. *closes*] cadences. 35. *idleness*] worthlessness.
[III.v]
5. *feed*] bribed.

awry; who being slain, supposed by thine own hands, 15
defended by his sword, made thee most loathsome, him
most gracious with thy loose princess; thou, closely yielding
egress and regress to her, madest him heir whose hot unquiet
lust straight tous'd thy sheets and now would seize thy state.
Politician! Wise man! Death! To be led to the stake like a 20
bull by the horns; to make even kindness cut a gentle throat!
Life, why art thou numbed? Thou foggy dullness, speak!
Lives not more faith in a home-thrusting tongue than in these
fencing tip-tap courtiers?

Enter Celso, *with a hermit's gown and beard.*

PIETRO.

Lord Malevole, if this be true— 25

MALEVOLE.

If! Come, shade thee with this disguise. If! Thou shalt handle
it; he shall thank thee for killing thyself. Come, follow my
directions, and thou shalt see strange sleights.

PIETRO.

World, whither wilt thou?

MALEVOLE.

Why, to the devil. Come, the morn grows late. 30
A steady quickness is the soul of state. *Exeunt.*

[IV.i] *Enter* Maquerelle, *knocking at the Ladies' door.*

MAQUERELLE.

Medam, medam, are you stirring, medam? If you be
stirring, medam—if I thought I should disturb ye—

[*Enter* Page.]

PAGE.

My lady is up, forsooth.

MAQUERELLE.

A pretty boy, faith. How old art thou?

25. S.P. PIETRO.] *Dyce; Cel. Qq.*
[IV.i]
2.1.] *Dyce.*

---

17. *closely*] secretly. 19. *tous'd*] disheveled.
24. *tip-tap*] light-thrusting (B-H-N). 31. *state*] statecraft (Spencer).
[IV.i]
1. *Medam*] probably affected pronunciation.

PAGE.

I think fourteen. 5

MAQUERELLE.

Nay, and ye be in the teens—Are ye a gentleman born? Do you know me? My name is Medam Maquerelle; I lie in the old Cunnycourt. —See, here the ladies.

Enter Biancha *and* Emilia.

BIANCHA.

A fair day to ye, Maquerelle.

EMILIA.

Is the duchess up yet, sentinel? 10

MAQUERELLE.

O ladies, the most abominable mischance! O dear ladies, the most piteous disaster! Ferneze was taken last night in the duchess' chamber. Alas, the duke catch'd him and kill'd him.

BIANCHA.

Was he found in bed? 15

MAQUERELLE.

O, no; but the villainous certainty is, the door was not bolted, the tongue-tied hatch held his peace; so the naked troth is, he was found in his shirt whilst I like an arrant beast lay in the outward chamber, heard nothing; and yet they came by me in the dark, and yet I felt them not, like 20 a senseless creature as I was. O beauties, look to your busk-points, if not chastely, yet charily: be sure the door be bolted. —Is your lord gone to Florence?

BIANCHA.

Yes, Maquerelle.

MAQUERELLE.

I hope you'll find the discretion to purchase a fresh gown 25 for his return. —Now, by my troth, beauties, I would ha' ye once wise. He loves ye; pish! He is witty; bubble! Fair-proportioned; meaw! Nobly-born; wind! Let this be still your fix'd position: esteem me every man according to his

7. *lie*] lodge.
8. *Cunnycourt*] quarters for women (B-H-N).
17. *hatch*] half-door. 22. *busk-points*] stays, laces.

good gifts, and so ye shall ever remain most dear and most worthy to be most dear ladies. 30

EMILIA.

Is the duke return'd from hunting yet?

MAQUERELLE.

They say not yet.

BIANCHA.

'Tis now in midst of day.

EMILIA.

How bears the duchess with this blemish now? 35

MAQUERELLE.

Faith, boldly; strongly defies defame, as one that has a duke to her father. And there's a note to you: be sure of a stout friend in a corner that may always awe your husband. Mark the 'havior of the duchess now; she dares defame; cries, "Duke, do what thou canst, I'll quit mine honor." 40 Nay, as one confirmed in her own virtue against ten thousand mouths that mutter her disgrace, she's presently for dances.

Enter Ferrardo.

BIANCHA.

For dances!

MAQUERELLE.

Most true. 45

EMILIA.

Most strange. [*Aside to* Maquerelle.] See, here's my servant, young Ferrard. How many servants think'st thou I have, Maquerelle?

MAQUERELLE [*aside to* Emilia].

The more, the merrier. 'Twas well said, use your servants as you do your smocks; have many, use one, and change 50 often, for that's most sweet and courtlike.

FERRARDO.

Save ye, fair ladies! Is the duke returned?

46–48.] *Neilson suggests speech probably belongs to Biancha.*

30–31. *most . . . ladies*] from Sidney's Dedication of the *Arcadia* (B-P).
36. *defame*] infamy. 37. *note*] observation.
39. *dares*] defies. 40. *quit*] acquit.

BIANCHA.

Sweet sir, no voice of him as yet in court.

FERRARDO.

'Tis very strange.

BIANCHA [*aside to* Maquerelle].

And how like you my servant, Maquerelle? 55

MAQUERELLE [*aside to* Biancha].

I think he could hardly draw Ulysses' bow; but, by my fidelity, were his nose narrower, his eyes broader, his hands thinner, his lips thicker, his legs bigger, his feet lesser, his hair blacker, and his teeth whiter, he were a tolerable sweet youth, i'faith. And he will come to my chamber, I will read 60 him the fortune of his beard.

Cornets sound.

FERRARDO.

Not yet return'd! I fear—But the duchess approacheth.

[IV.ii]

Enter Mendoza *supporting the* Duchess, Guerrino; *the Ladies that are on the stage rise;* Ferrardo *ushers in the* Duchess, *and then takes a Lady to tread a measure.*

AURELIA.

We will dance. Music! We will dance.

GUERRINO.

Les quanto, lady, *Pensez bien*, *Passa regis*, or Biancha's Brawl?

AURELIA.

We have forgot the brawl.

FERRARDO.

So soon? 'Tis wonder. 5

GUERRINO.

Why, 'tis but two singles on the left, two on the right, three doubles forward, a traverse of six round; do this

7. doubles] *Q*, *Q2;* double *Q1*.

0.3. *measure*] solemn, stately dance.

2–3. *Les quanto . . . Brawl*] names of dances; the brawl was introduced from France about the mid-sixteenth century.

twice, three singles side, galliard trick-of-twenty, coranto-pace; a figure of eight, three singles broken down, come up, meet, two doubles, fall back, and then honor. 10

AURELIA.

O Dædalus, thy maze! I have quite forgot it.

MAQUERELLE.

Trust me, so have I, saving the falling back and then honor.

Enter Prepasso.

AURELIA.

Music, music!

PREPASSO.

Who saw the duke? The duke?

Enter Equato.

AURELIA.

Music! 15

EQUATO.

The duke? Is the duke returned?

AURELIA.

Music!

Enter Celso.

CELSO.

The duke is either quite invisible or else is not.

AURELIA.

We are not pleased with your intrusion upon our private retirement; we are not pleased. You have forgot yourselves. 20

Enter a Page.

CELSO.

Boy, thy master? Where's the duke?

PAGE.

Alas, I left him burying the earth with his spread, joyless limbs. He told me he was heavy, would sleep; bid me walk off, for that the strength of fantasy oft made him talk in his

16. S.P. EQUATO.] *Q1; E. Q2; Pre: Q.*

23. bid] *Q;* bade *Q1–2.*

24. talk] *Q, Q2;* talking *Q1.*

---

8. *galliard trick-of-twenty*] The galliard is a lively dance with five steps to a phrase; trick-of-twenty is probably some variant of it.

8–9. *coranto-pace*] swift-paced courtly dance, characterized by a running glide.

10. *honor*] curtsy.

12. *saving . . . honor*] *double entendre,* of course.

dreams. I straight obeyed, nor ever saw him since; but, 25
wheresoe'er he is, he's sad.

AURELIA.

Music, sound high, as is our heart! Sound high!

[IV.iii] *Enter* Malevole, *and* Pietro *disguised like an hermit*

MALEVOLE.

The duke—peace!—the duke is dead.

AURELIA.

Music!

MALEVOLE.

Is't music?

MENDOZA.

Give proof.

FERRARDO.

How? 5

CELSO.

Where?

PREPASSO.

When?

MALEVOLE.

Rest in peace, as the duke does; quietly sit. For my own
part, I beheld him but dead; that's all. Marry, here's one
can give you a more particular account of him. 10

MENDOZA.

Speak, holy father, nor let any brow
Within this presence fright thee from the truth.
Speak confidently and freely.

AURELIA. We attend.

PIETRO.

Now had the mounting sun's all-ripening wings
Swept the cold sweat of night from earth's dank breast, 15
When I, whom men call Hermit of the Rock,
Forsook my cell and clamber'd up a cliff,
Against whose base the heady Neptune dash'd
His high-curl'd brows; there 'twas I eas'd my limbs

25. ever] *Q, Q2;* neuer *Q1.*

[IV.iii]
11–13.] *Dyce; as prose Qq.*

When, lo, my entrails melted with the moan 20
Someone, who far 'bove me was climb'd, did make—
I shall offend—

MENDOZA.

Not.

AURELIA.

On.

PIETRO.

Methinks I hear him yet: "O female faith! 25
Go sow the ingrateful sand, and love a woman!
And do I live to be the scoff of men?
To be the wittol-cuckold, even to hug my poison?
Thou knowest, O truth,
Sooner hard steel will melt with southern wind, 30
A seaman's whistle calm the ocean,
A town on fire be extinct with tears,
Than women, vow'd to blushless impudence,
With sweet behavior and soft minioning
Will turn from that where appetite is fix'd. 35
O powerful blood! how thou dost slave their soul!
I wash'd an Ethiope, who, for recompense,
Sullied my name. And must I, then, be forc'd
To walk, to live thus black? Must! Must! Fie!
He that can bare with 'must,' he cannot die." 40
With that he sigh'd so passionately deep
That the dull air even groan'd. At last he cries,
"Sink shame in seas, sink deep enough!" so dies,
For then I view'd his body fall and souse
Into the foamy main. O, then I saw 45
That which methinks I see: it was the duke,
Whom straight the nicer-stomach'd sea
Belch'd up, but then—

MALEVOLE.

Then came I in; but, 'las, all was too late,

28. the] *Q;* their *Q1–2.* 41. so] *Q1;* too *Q, Q2.*

---

32. *fire*] dissyllabic (Spencer). 32. *extinct*] extinguished.
34. *minioning*] to treat as a minion; caressing.
44. *souse*] "fall with violence—the word is used of a hawk swooping down on its prey" (Bullen).

For even straight he sunk!

PIETRO. Such was the duke's sad fate. 50

CELSO.
A better fortune to our Duke Mendoza!

OMNES.
Mendoza! *Cornets flourish.*

MENDOZA.
A guard, a guard!

Enter a Guard.

We, full of hearty tears,
For our good father's loss—
For so we well may call him 55
Who did beseech your loves for our succession—
Cannot so lightly overjump his death
As leave his woes revengeless. —(*To* Aurelia.)
Woman of shame,
We banish thee forever to the place
From whence this good man comes; nor permit, 60
On death, unto the body any ornament;
But base, as was thy life, depart away.

AURELIA.
Ungrateful!

MENDOZA. Away!

AURELIA. Villain, hear me!

Prepasso *and* Guerrino *lead away the* Duchess.

MENDOZA. Begone!—
My lords, address to public council; 'tis most fit
The train of Fortune is borne up by wit. 65
Away! Our presence shall be sudden; haste.

All depart saving Mendoza, Malevole, *and* Pietro.

MALEVOLE.
Now, you egregious devil! Ha, ye murdering politician!

52. S.P. OMNES.] *Q, Q2;* Cry all, *Q1.*
53. A . . . guard!] *after S.D., Q.*
58. S.D.] *Q, Q2;* To *Emilia Q1.*

53.] Mendoza immediately assumes the royal "we"; cf. Malevole at IV.v.129.
57. *overjump*] pass over.
64. *address to*] prepare for.
67. *politician*] schemer.

How dost, duke? How dost look now? Brave duke, i'faith!

MENDOZA.

How did you kill him?

MALEVOLE.

Slatted his brains out, then sous'd him in the briny sea. 70

MENDOZA.

Brain'd him, and drown'd him too?

MALEVOLE.

O, 'twas best, sure work; for he that strikes a great man, let him strike home, or else 'ware he'll prove no man. Shoulder not a huge fellow unless you may be sure to lay him in the kennel. 75

MENDOZA.

A most sound brainpan! I'll make you both emperors.

MALEVOLE.

Make us Christians, make us Christians!

MENDOZA.

I'll hoist ye; ye shall mount.

MALEVOLE.

To the gallows, say ye? Come! "*Præmium incertum petit certum scelus.*" How stands the progress? 80

MENDOZA.

Here, take my ring unto the citadel;
Have entrance to Maria, the grave duchess
Of banish'd Altofront. Tell her we love her;
Omit no circumstance to grace our person; do't.

MALEVOLE.

I'll make an excellent pander. Duke, farewell; 'dieu, adieu, duke. 85

MENDOZA.

Take Maquerelle with thee, for 'tis found

79. Come!] *Q, Q2;* O ô me *Q1.* 85. I'll] *Q;* Iste *Q1–2.*

---

70. *Slatted*] dashed.
75. *kennel*] gutter.
79–80. *Præmium . . . scelus*] "Uncertain is the prize he seeks, certain is the crime" (Seneca *Phoenissæ* 632–633).
80. *progress*] course of action. 84. *circumstance*] detail.

None cuts a diamond but a diamond. *Exit* Malevole.
Hermit, thou art a man for me, my confessor.
O thou selected spirit, born for my good, 90
Sure thou wouldst make
An excellent elder in a deform'd church.
Come, we must be inward, thou and I all one.

PIETRO.
I am glad I was ordained for ye.

MENDOZA.
Go to, then; thou must know that Malevole is a strange 95
villain; dangerous, very dangerous. You see how broad 'a
speaks; a gross-jaw'd rogue. I would have thee poison him;
he's like a corn upon my great toe—I cannot go for him;
he must be cored out, he must. Wilt do't, ha?

PIETRO.
Anything, anything. 100

MENDOZA.
Heart of my life! Thus, then, to the citadel.
Thou shalt consort with this Malevole;
There being at supper, poison him. It shall be laid
Upon Maria, who yields love or dies.
Scud quick like lightning! 105

PIETRO.
Good deeds crawl, but mischief flies. *Exit* Pietro.

Enter Malevole.

MALEVOLE.
Your devilship's ring has no virtue: the buff-captain, the
sallow Westphalian gammon-faced zaza, cries, "Stand out!
Must have a stiffer warrant, or no pass into the Castle of
Comfort." 110

88. S.D.] *after l. 86 Q, Q2; not in Q1.*

105. like lightning!] *Q; part of Pietro's speech (l. 106) Q1; with l. 106, part of Mendoza's speech Q2.*

---

92. *deform'd church*] irregular, i.e., Puritan.
93. *inward*] intimate.
96. *broad 'a*] outspokenly he.
98. *go for him*] walk because of him.
107. *buff-captain*] referring to the buff or leather jerkin that he wears.
108. *gammon-faced*] pig-faced; the western German province of Westphalia was associated with bacon or gammon (*OED*).
108. *zaza*] bully (B-P; Spencer conjectures *Saxon*)?

MENDOZA.

Command our sudden letter. —Not enter! Sha't! What place is there in Genoa but thou shalt? Into my heart, into my very heart! Come, let's love; we must love, we two, soul and body.

MALEVOLE.

How didst like the hermit? A strange hermit, sirrah. 115

MENDOZA.

A dangerous fellow, very perilous. He must die.

MALEVOLE.

Ay, he must die.

MENDOZA.

Thou'st kill him. We are wise; we must be wise.

MALEVOLE.

And provident.

MENDOZA.

Yea, provident. Beware an hypocrite; 120
A churchman once corrupted, O, avoid!

Shoots under his belly.

A fellow that makes religion his stalking-horse,
He breeds a plague. Thou shalt poison him.

MALEVOLE.

Ho, 'tis wondrous necessary; how?

MENDOZA.

You both go jointly to the citadel; 125
There sup, there poison him; and Maria,
Because she is our opposite, shall bear
The sad suspect—on which she dies or loves us.

MALEVOLE.

I run. *Exit* Malevole.

121.1.] *Q, Q2; not in Q1.*

---

111. *Sha't!*] Thou shalt! 118. *Thou'st*] Thou must.

121.1 *Shoots . . . belly*] "manner in which a corrupt churchman makes religion his stalking-horse, viz., by shooting at his object under its belly" (Collier).

122. *stalking-horse*] "a horse trained to allow a fowler to conceal himself behind it or under its coverings in order to get within easy range of the game without alarming it"; hence, "an underhand means or expedient for making an attack or attaining some sinister object" (*OED*).

128. *sad*] weighty.

MENDOZA.

We that are great, our sole self-good still moves us. 130
They shall die both, for their deserts craves more
Than we can recompense; their presence still
Imbraids our fortunes with beholdingness,
Which we abhor; like deed, not doer. Then conclude,
They live not to cry out, "Ingratitude!" 135
One stick burns t'other; steel cuts steel alone.
'Tis good trust few; but, O, 'tis best trust none.

Exit Mendoza.

[IV.iv] *Enter* Malevole *and* Pietro *still disguised, at several doors.*

MALEVOLE.

How do you? How dost, duke?

PIETRO.

O, let the last day fall! Drop, drop on our cursed heads!
Let heaven unclasp itself, vomit forth flames.

MALEVOLE.

O, do not rand, do not turn player. There's more of them than can well live one by another already. What, art an infidel still? 5

PIETRO.

I am amaz'd, struck in a swoon with wonder. I am commanded to poison thee.

MALEVOLE.

I am commanded to poison thee at supper.

PIETRO.

At supper? 10

MALEVOLE.

In the citadel.

PIETRO.

In the citadel?

2. on] *Q; in Q1–2.*
4. rand] *Q, Q2;* raue *Q1.*
7. amaz'd] *Q, Q2;* mazde *Q1.*

133. *Imbraids*] upbraids.
133. *beholdingness*] obligation or indebtedness.
[IV.iv]
4. *rand*] rant.

MALEVOLE.

Cross-capers! Tricks! Truth o' heaven! He would discharge us as boys do eldern guns, one pellet to strike out another. Of what faith art now? 15

PIETRO.

All is damnation, wickedness extreme. There is no faith in man.

MALEVOLE.

In none but usurers and brokers; they deceive no man. Men take 'em for bloodsuckers, and so they are! Now God deliver me from my friends! 20

PIETRO.

Thy friends!

MALEVOLE.

Yes, from my friends, for from mine enemies I'll deliver myself. O, cutthroat friendship is the rankest villainy! Mark this Mendoza; mark him for a villain; but heaven will send a plague upon him for a rogue. 25

PIETRO.

O world!

MALEVOLE.

World! 'Tis the only region of death, the greatest shop of the devil, the cruel'st prison of men, out of the which none pass without paying their dearest breath for a fee. There's nothing perfect in it but extreme, extreme calamity, such as comes yonder. 30

[IV.v]

Enter Aurelia, *two Halberds before and two after, supported by* Celso *and* Ferrardo; Aurelia *in base mourning attire.*

AURELIA.

To banishment! Led on to banishment!

13. He] *Q, Q2; not in Q1.*
14. eldern] *Q, Q2;* elder *Q1.*
18. S.P. MALEVOLE.] *Dyce; Men. Qq.*

---

13. *Cross-capers*] steps in dancing; here, tricks.
14. *eldern guns*] made of elderwood, i.e., popguns.

[IV.v]

0.1. *Halberds*] halberdiers.

PIETRO.

Lady, the blessedness of repentance to you!

AURELIA.

Why? why? I can desire nothing but death,
Nor deserve anything but hell.
If heaven should give sufficiency of grace 5
To clear my soul, it would make heaven graceless:
My sins would make the stock of mercy poor.
O, they would tire heaven's goodness to reclaim them!
Judgment is just yet from that vast villain.
But, sure, he shall not miss sad punishment 10
'Fore he shall rule. —On to my cell of shame.

PIETRO.

My cell 'tis, lady, where, instead of masques,
Music, tilts, tourneys, and such courtlike shows,
The hollow murmur of the checkless winds
Shall groan again, whilst the unquiet sea 15
Shakes the whole rock with foamy battery.
There usherless the air comes in and out;
The rheumy vault will force your eyes to weep,
Whilst you behold true desolation.
A rocky barrenness shall pierce your eyes, 20
Where all at once one reaches where he stands,
With brows the roof, both walls with both his hands.

AURELIA.

It is too good. —Blessed spirit of my lord,
O, in what orb soe'er thy soul is thron'd,
Behold me worthily most miserable! 25
O, let the anguish of my contrite spirit
Entreat some reconciliation!
If not, O, joy, triumph in my just grief!
Death is the end of woes and tears' relief.

8. tire] *Q, Q2;* try *Q1.* 20. pierce] *Q, Q2;* pain *Q1.*

---

9. *yet*] even.
16. *battery*] battering.
17. *usherless*] "*i.e.* without the ceremony of an Usher to give notice of its approach, as is usual in Courts" (Charles Lamb, *Specimens of English Dramatic Poets* [London, 1893], I, 186).
18. *rheumy*] damp.

PIETRO.

Belike your lord not lov'd you, was unkind. 30

AURELIA.

O heaven!
As the soul lov'd the body, so lov'd he.
'Twas death to him to part my presence; heaven,
To see me pleased.
Yet I, like to a wretch given o'er to hell, 35
Brake all the sacred rites of marriage
To clip a base, ungentle, faithless villain.
O God, a very pagan reprobate—
What should I say?—ungrateful, throws me out,
For whom I lost soul, body, fame, and honor. 40
But 'tis most fit: why should a better fate
Attend on any who forsake chaste sheets,
Fly the embrace of a devoted heart,
Join'd by a solemn vow 'fore God and man,
To taste the brackish blood of beastly lust 45
In an adulterous touch? O ravenous immodesty!
Insatiate impudence of appetite!
Look, here's your end; for mark, what sap in dust,
What sin in good, even so much love in lust.
Joy to thy ghost, sweet lord! Pardon to me! 50

CELSO.

'Tis the duke's pleasure this night you rest in court.

AURELIA.

Soul, lurk in shades; run, shame, from brightsome skies,
In night the blind man misseth not his eyes.

Exit [*with* Celso, Ferrardo, *and Halberds*].

MALEVOLE.

Do not weep, kind cuckold; take comfort, man; thy betters have been *beccos*: Agamemnon, emperor of all the merry 55 Greeks, that tickled all the true Trojans, was a *cornuto*; Prince Arthur, that cut off twelve kings' beards, was a *cornuto*;

53.1. *with . . . Halberds*] *Dyce.*

---

32. *soul lov'd*] i.e., loved and loves (emphatic).
45. *brackish*] salt, lascivious.
46. *immodesty*] excess.
47. *impudence*] shamelessness (B-P).

Hercules, whose back bore up heaven, and got forty wenches with child in one night—

PIETRO.

Nay, 'twas fifty. 60

MALEVOLE.

Faith, forty's enow, o' conscience—yet was a *cornuto*. Patience; mischief grows proud; be wise.

PIETRO.

Thou pinchest too deep, art too keen upon me.

MALEVOLE.

Tut, a pitiful surgeon makes a dangerous sore; I'll tent thee to the ground. Thinkest I'll sustain myself by flattering thee 65 because thou art a prince? I had rather follow a drunkard, and live by licking up his vomit, than by servile flattery.

PIETRO.

Yet great men ha' done't.

MALEVOLE.

Great slaves fear better than love, born naturally for a coal basket, though the common usher of princes' presence, 70 Fortune, hath blindly given them better place. I am vowed to be thy affliction.

PIETRO.

Prithee, be; I love much misery, and be thou son to me.

Enter Bilioso.

MALEVOLE.

Because you are an usurping duke. —(*To* Bilioso.) Your lordship's well return'd from Florence. 75

BILIOSO.

Well return'd, I praise my horse.

MALEVOLE.

What news from the Florentines?

BILIOSO.

I will conceal the great duke's pleasure; only this was his

71. hath] *Q*; ha *Q1–2*. 75. from] *Q*, *Q2*; for *Q1*.

58–59. *and got . . . night*] legend has fifty.

64. *tent*] probe. ("Wounds were probed, then 'tented,' i.e. cleaned out with lint. The too sympathetic surgeon spares the patient pain but leaves the wound foul"—Harrison.)

69–70. *for a coal basket*] for servile tasks.

charge: his pleasure is that his daughter die, Duke Pietro be banished for banishing his blood's dishonor, and that Duke Altofront be reaccepted. This is all. But I hear Duke Pietro is dead. 80

MALEVOLE.
Ay, and Mendoza is duke. What will you do?

BILIOSO.
Is Mendoza strongest?

MALEVOLE.
Yet he is. 85

BILIOSO.
Then yet I'll hold with him.

MALEVOLE.
But if that Altofront should turn straight again?

BILIOSO.
Why, then, I would turn straight again.
'Tis good run still with him that has most might:
I had rather stand with wrong than fall with right. 90

MALEVOLE.
What religion will you be of now?

BILIOSO.
Of the duke's religion, when I know what it is.

MALEVOLE.
O Hercules!

BILIOSO.
Hercules? Hercules was the son of Jupiter and Alcmena.

MALEVOLE.
Your lordship is a very wittol. 95

BILIOSO.
Wittol?

MALEVOLE.
Ay, all-wit.

BILIOSO.
Amphitryo was a cuckold.

91–98.] *addition Q, Q2; not in Q1.*
91. What] *Q, Q2 (corrected)*; Of what *Q2 (uncorrected)*.
98.] *Q2 (uncorrected) repeats l. 90 after this line.*

---

80. *banishing*] "may stand in the sense of: 'for [the purpose of] banishing his dishonoured blood'" (Wood).
87. *turn straight again*] return straightway (B-H-N).

MALEVOLE.

Your lordship sweats; your young lady will get you a cloth
for your old worship's brows. *Exit* Bilioso. 100
Here's a fellow to be damned! This is his inviolable maxim:
Flatter the greatest and oppress the least. A whoreson
flesh-fly, that still gnaws upon the lean, gall'd backs!

PIETRO.

Why dost, then, salute him?

MALEVOLE.

I'faith, as bawds go to church—for fashion sake. Come, 105
be not confounded; thou art but in danger to lose a duke-
dom. Think this: this earth is the only grave and Golgotha
wherein all things that live must rot; 'tis but the draught
wherein the heavenly bodies discharge their corruption;
the very muck hill on which the sublunary orbs cast their 110
excrements. Man is the slime of this dung pit, and princes
are the governors of these men; for, for our souls, they are as
free as emperors, all of one piece; there goes but a pair of
shears betwixt an emperor and the son of a bagpiper—only
the dyeing, dressing, pressing, glossing makes the difference. 115
Now what art thou like to lose?
A jailer's office to keep men in bonds,
Whilst toil and treason all life's good confounds.

PIETRO.

I here renounce forever regency.
O Altofront, I wrong thee to supplant thy right, 120
To trip thy heels up with a devilish sleight;
For which I now from throne am thrown, world-tricks
abjure;
For vengeance, though 't comes slow, yet it comes sure.
O, I am chang'd. For here, 'fore the dread power,
In true contrition I do dedicate 125
My breath to solitary holiness,
My lips to prayer, and my breast's care shall be
Restoring Altofront to regency.

103. lean] *not in Q2* (*uncorrected*).
105. I'faith] *Q;* Faith *Q1–2.*
106. thou art] *Q;* th'art *Q1–2.*
123. though 't] *Q*, *Q2*; that *Q1.*

---

108. *draught*] privy.
113–114. *there goes . . . shears*] cut of the same cloth (proverbial).
115. *glossing*] finishing (B-P). 118. *confounds*] overthrows.

MALEVOLE.
Thy vows are heard, and we accept thy faith.
Undisguiseth himself.

Enter Ferneze *and* Celso.

Banish amazement. Come, we four must stand 130
Full shock of Fortune. Be not no wonder-stricken.

PIETRO.
Doth Ferneze live?

FERNEZE. For your pardon.

PIETRO.
Pardon and love. Give leave to recollect
My thoughts dispers'd in wild astonishment.
My vows stand fix'd in heaven, and from hence 135
I crave all love and pardon.

MALEVOLE. Who doubts of Providence,
That sees this change? A hearty faith to all!
He needs must rise who can no lower fall:
For still impetuous vicissitude
Touseth the world; then let no maze intrude 140
Upon your spirits. Wonder not I rise,
For who can sink that close can temporize?
The time grows ripe for action. I'll detect
My privat'st plot, lest ignorance fear suspect.
Let's close to counsel, leave the rest to fate; 145
Mature discretion is the life of state. *Exeunt.*

[V.i] *Enter* Bilioso *and* Passarello.

BILIOSO.
Fool, how dost thou like my calf in a long stocking?

PASSARELLO.
An excellent calf, my lord.

129.2.] *Qq add "Altofront, Ferneze, Celso, Pietro."*
138. who] *Q1–2; not in Q.*
140. Touseth] *Q, Q2;* Looseth *Q1.*
[V.i]
V.i.] *addition Q.*

140. *Touseth*] cf. III.iii.59.
143. *detect*] expose.

BILIOSO.

This calf hath been a reveler this twenty year. When Monsieur Gundi lay here ambassador, I could have carried a lady up and down at arms' end in a platter; and 5
I can tell you, there were those at that time who, to try the strength of a man's back and his arm, would be coister'd. I have measured calves with most of the palace, and they come nothing near me; besides, I think there be not many armors in the arsenal will fit me, especially for the headpiece. 10
I'll tell thee—

PASSARELLO.

What, my lord?

BILIOSO.

I can eat stew'd broth as it comes seething off the fire, or a custard as it comes reeking out of the oven; and I think there are not many lords can do it. [*Displaying his pomander.*] A good pomander, a little decayed in the scent, 15
but six grains of musk, ground with rosewater and temper'd with a little civet, shall fetch her again presently.

PASSARELLO.

O, ay, as a bawd with aqua vitae.

BILIOSO.

And, what, dost thou rail upon the ladies as thou wert 20
wont?

PASSARELLO.

I were better roast a live cat, and might do it with more safety. I am as secret to the thieves as their painting. There's Maquerelle, oldest bawd and a perpetual beggar. Did you never hear of her trick to be known in the city? 25

BILIOSO.

Never.

15–16. S.D.] *B-H-N.* 23. the] *Bullen; not in Q.*

7. *coister'd*] "coiled up into a small compass" (*OED*, quoting Nares' *Glossary*); inconvenienced (Halliwell); possibly *hoistered*, meaning supported (E. K. Deighton, *The Old Dramatists: Conjectural Readings* [Westminster, 1896]).

15–16. S.D. *pomander*] a perfume ball carried in the pocket or worn around the neck.

18. *fetch her*] i.e., restore its efficacy (Spencer).

PASSARELLO.

Why, she gets all the picture-makers to draw her picture; when they have done, she most courtly finds fault with them one after another, and never fetcheth them. They, in revenge of this, execute her in pictures as they do in Germany, and hang her in their shops. By this means is she better known to the stinkards than if she had been five times carted. 30

BILIOSO.

'Fore God, an excellent policy.

PASSARELLO.

Are there any revels tonight, my lord?

BILIOSO.

Yes. 35

PASSARELLO.

Good, my lord, give me leave to break a fellow's pate that hath abused me.

BILIOSO.

Whose pate?

PASSARELLO.

Young Ferrard, my lord.

BILIOSO.

Take heed; he's very valiant. I have known him fight eight quarrels in five days, believe it. 40

PASSARELLO.

O, is he so great a quarreler? Why, then, he's an arrant coward.

BILIOSO.

How prove you that?

PASSARELLO.

Why, thus: he that quarrels seeks to fight; and he that seeks to fight seeks to die; and he that seeks to die seeks never to fight more; and he that will quarrel and seeks means never to answer a man more, I think he's a coward. 45

BILIOSO.

Thou canst prove anything.

---

32. *stinkards*] stinking fellows (Neilson).

32. *carted*] referring to the practice of carting bawds around London as a punishment.

PASSARELLO.

Anything but a rich knave, for I can flatter no man. 50

BILIOSO.

Well, be not drunk, good fool. I shall see you anon in the presence. [*Exeunt.*]

[V.ii]

Enter Malevole *and* Maquerelle, *at several doors opposite, singing.*

MALEVOLE.

"The Dutchman for a drunkard,"—

MAQUERELLE.

"The Dane for golden locks,"—

MALEVOLE.

"The Irishman for usquebaugh,"—

MAQUERELLE.

"The Frenchman for the (   )."

MALEVOLE.

O, thou art a blessed creature! Had I a modest woman 5
to conceal, I would put her to thy custody; for no reasonable creature would ever suspect her to be in thy company. Ha, thou art a melodious Maquerelle, thou picture of a woman and substance of a beast!

Enter Passarello.

MAQUERELLE.

O fool, will ye be ready anon to go with me to the revels? 10
The hall will be so pester'd anon.

PASSARELLO.

Ay, as the country is with attorneys.

MALEVOLE.

What hast thou there, fool?

PASSARELLO.

Wine. I have learn'd to drink since I went with my lord

52. S.D. *Exeunt.*] *Dodsley; Exit. Q.* V.ii.] *Dyce; no scene division in Q.* 9.1–39.] *addition Q.*

---

51. *anon*] immediately, at once.

[V.ii]

3. *usquebaugh*] whiskey.

4. (   )] rhyme word is obvious. 11. *pester'd*] overcrowded.

ambassador. I'll drink to the health of Madam Maquerelle. 15

MALEVOLE.

Why, thou wast wont to rail upon her.

PASSARELLO.

Ay, but since I borrow'd money of her, I'll drink to her health now, as gentlemen visit brokers, or as knights send venison to the city, either to take up more money or to procure longer forbearance. 20

MALEVOLE.

Give me the bowl. I drink a health to Altofront, our deposed duke. [*Drinks.*]

PASSARELLO.

I'll take it. [*Drinks.*] So! Now I'll begin a health to Madam Maquerelle. [*Drinks.*]

MALEVOLE.

Pugh! I will not pledge her. 25

PASSARELLO.

Why, I pleg'd your lord.

MALEVOLE.

I care not.

PASSARELLO.

Not pledge Madam Maquerelle! Why, then, will I spew up your lord again with this fool's finger.

MALEVOLE.

Hold; I'll take it. [*Drinks.*] 30

MAQUERELLE.

Now thou hast drunk my health, fool, I am friends with thee.

PASSARELLO.

Art? art?

When Griffon saw the reconciled quean
Offering about his neck her arms to cast, 35
He threw off sword and heart's malignant stream,
And lovely her below the loins embrac'd.

17–20.] *Dodsley; as verse Q.*
22, 23, 24. S.D.] *Dyce.*
30. S.D.] *Dyce.*

34–37. *When . . . embrac'd*] source of the lines not known. Griffon is a hero in Ariosto's *Orlando Furioso*.

34. *quean*] hussy; bawd.

Adieu, Madame Maquerelle. *Exit* Passarello.

MALEVOLE.

And how dost thou think o' this transformation of state now?

MAQUERELLE.

Verily, very well; for we women always note the falling of 40
the one is the rising of the other; some must be fat, some
must be lean; some must be fools, and some must be lords;
some must be knaves, and some must be officers; some must
be beggars, some must be knights; some must be cuckolds,
and some must be citizens. As for example, I have two court 45
dogs, the most fawning curs, the one called Watch, th'
other Catch. Now I, like Lady Fortune, sometimes love
this dog, sometimes raise that dog, sometimes favor Watch,
most commonly fancy Catch. Now that dog which I favor I
feed; and he's so ravenous that what I give he never chaws 50
it, gulps it down whole, without any relish of what he has,
but with a greedy expectation of what he shall have. The
other dog now—

MALEVOLE.

No more dog, sweet Maquerelle, no more dog. And what
hope hast thou of the Duchess Maria? Will she stoop to 55
the duke's lure? Will she come, think'st?

MAQUERELLE. Let me see, where's the sign now? Ha' ye e'er a
calendar? Where's the sign, trow you?

MALEVOLE.

Sign! Why, is there any moment in that?

MAQUERELLE.

O, believe me, a most secret power. Look ye, a Chaldean 60
or an Assyrian, I am sure 'twas a most sweet Jew, told me,
court any woman in the right sign, you shall not miss. But
you must take her in the right vein then, as, when the sign
is in Pisces, a fishmonger's wife is very sociable; in Cancer,

40. Verily, very] *Q*, *Q2;* Verie verie *Q1.*
46. the most] *Q*, *Q2;* most *Q1.*
48. raise] *Q*, *Q2;* rouse *Q1.*
56. come] *Q1–2;* cowe *Q*.

---

56. *lure*] enticement; term from falconry to denote the apparatus used by falconers to recall hawks (*OED*).
56. *come*] yield; be favorably moved.
58. *sign*] astrological sign of the zodiac (B-P).

a Precisian's wife is very flexible; in Capricorn, a merchant's wife hardly holds out; in Libra, a lawyer's wife is very tractable, especially if her husband be at the term; only in Scorpio 'tis very dangerous meddling. Has the duke sent any jewel, any rich stones? 65

Enter Captain.

MALEVOLE.

Ay, I think those are the best signs to take a lady in. —By your favor, signior, I must discourse with the Lady Maria, Altofront's duchess; I must enter for the duke. 70

CAPTAIN.

She here shall give you interview. I received the guardship of this citadel from the good Altofront, and for his use I'll keep't till I am of no use. 75

MALEVOLE.

Wilt thou? O heavens, that a Christian should be found in a buff-jerkin! Captain Conscience, I love thee, captain. We attend. (*Exit* Captain.) —And what hope hast thou of this duchess' easiness?

MAQUERELLE.

'Twill go hard. She was a cold creature ever; she hated monkeys, fools, jesters, and gentlemen ushers extremely; she had the vile trick on't, not only to be truly modestly honorable in her own conscience, but she would avoid the least wanton carriage that might incur suspect, as, God bless me, she had almost brought bed-pressing out of fashion. I could scarce get a fine for the lease of a lady's favor once in a fortnight. 80 85

MALEVOLE.

Now, in the name of immodesty, how many maidenheads hast thou brought to the block?

MAQUERELLE.

Let me see. Heaven forgive us our misdeeds! —Here's the duchess. 90

76. heavens] *Q, Q2;* heaven *Q1.* 78. S.D.] *after* captain (*l. 77*) *Qq.*

---

65. *Precisian's*] Puritan's.
67. *term*] session of the law court. 70. *take . . . in*] overcome.
78. *attend*] await. 86. *fine*] fee.

[V.iii] *Enter* Maria *and* Captain.

MALEVOLE.
God bless thee, lady!

MARIA.
Out of thy company!

MALEVOLE.
We have brought thee tender of a husband.

MARIA.
I hope I have one already.

MAQUERELLE.
Nay, by mine honor, madam, as good ha' ne'er a husband as a banish'd husband; he's in another world now. I'll tell ye, lady, I have heard of a sect that maintained, when the husband was asleep, the wife might lawfully entertain another man, for then her husband was as dead—much more when he is banished! 5 10

MARIA.
Unhonest creature!

MAQUERELLE.
Pish, honesty is but an art to seem so. Pray ye, what's honesty, what's constancy, but fables feigned, odd old fools' chat, devised by jealous fools to wrong our liberty?

MALEVOLE.
Mully, he that loves thee is a duke, Mendoza. He will maintain thee royally, love thee ardently, defend thee powerfully, marry thee sumptuously, and keep thee in despite of Rosicleer or Donzel del Phoebo. There's jewels. [*Gives jewels.*] If thou wilt, so; if not, so. 15

MARIA.
Captain, for God's sake, save poor wretchedness 20
From tyranny of lustful insolence!
Enforce me in the deepest dungeon dwell
Rather than here; here round about is hell.—
O my dear'st Altofront, where'er thou breathe,
Let my soul sink into the shades beneath 25

18–19. S.D.] *B-H-N.* 20. sake] *Q;* loue *Q1–2.*

15. *Mully*] Molly; "term of endearment" (*OED*).

18. *Rosicleer or Donzel del Phoebo*] heroes of the popular romance, *The Mirror of Knighthood*, translated from the Spanish 1583–1601.

Before I stain thine honor! This thou hast,
And, long as I can die, I will live chaste.

MALEVOLE.

'Gainst him that can enforce, how vain is strife!

MARIA.

She that can be enforc'd has ne'er a knife;
She that through force her limbs with lust enrolls 30
Wants Cleopatra's asps and Portia's coals.
God amend you! *Exit with* Captain.

MALEVOLE.

Now, the fear of the devil forever go with thee! —Maquerelle, I tell thee, I have found an honest woman. Faith, I perceive, when all is done, there is of women, as of all other 35 things, some good, most bad; some saints, some sinners. For as nowadays no courtier but has his mistress, no captain but has his cockatrice, no cuckold but has his horns, and no fool but has his feather, even so, no woman but has her weakness and feather too, no sex but has his—I can hunt 40 the letter no farther. [*Aside.*] O God, how loathsome this toying is to me! That a duke should be forc'd to fool it! Well, "*Stultorum plena sunt omnia*": better play the fool lord than be the fool lord. —Now, where's your sleights, Madam Maquerelle? 45

MAQUERELLE.

Why, are ye ignorant that 'tis said a squeamish, affected niceness is natural to women, and that the excuse of their yielding is only, forsooth, the difficult obtaining? You must put her to't. Women are flax, and will fire in a moment. 50

MALEVOLE.

Why, was the flax put into thy mouth, and yet thou—thou set fire, thou inflame her?

26. This] *Q;* t'is *Q1–2.* 41. farther] *Q* (*farder*)*;* furder *Q1–2.*

38. *cockatrice*] mistress, whore; also, name of a fabled serpent.

40–41. *hunt the letter*] "pursue pretty parallels of alliterative phrasing in the manner of *Euphues*" (Harrison).

43. *Stultorum . . . omnia*] "Fools are everywhere" (from Cicero's *Epistolae ad Familiares* ix. 22).

47. *niceness*] coyness.

MAQUERELLE.

Marry, but I'll tell ye now, you were too hot.

MALEVOLE.

The fitter to have inflamed the flaxwoman.

MAQUERELLE.

You were too boisterous, spleeny, for, indeed— 55

MALEVOLE.

Go, go, thou art a weak pand'ress; now I see,
Sooner earth's fire heaven itself shall waste
Than all with heat can melt a mind that's chaste.
Go thou, the duke's lime-twig! I'll make the duke turn thee
out of thine office. What, not get one touch of hope, and had 60
her at such advantage!

MAQUERELLE.

Now, o' my conscience, now I think in my discretion, we did not take her in the right sign; the blood was not in the true vein, sure. *Exit*

Enter Bilioso.

BILIOSO.

Make way there! The duke returns from the enthronement. 65
—Malevole—

MALEVOLE.

Out, rogue!

BILIOSO.

Malevole—

MALEVOLE.

"Hence, ye gross-jaw'd, peasantly—out, go!"

BILIOSO.

Nay, sweet Malevole, since my return I hear you are 70
become the thing I always prophesied would be—an advanced virtue, a worthily-employed faithfulness, a man o' grace, dear friend. Come; what! "*Si quoties peccant homines*"—if as often as courtiers play the knaves, honest

64.1–96.] *addition Q.*

---

59. *lime-twig*] snare ("twig smeared with lime for catching birds" [*OED*]).
69. *Hence . . . go*] cf. II.iii.30.
73–74. *Si . . . homines*] "If as often as men sin," from Ovid's *Tristia* ii. 33, which continues: "Jupiter should hurl his thunderbolts, he would soon be weaponless."

men should be angry—why, look ye, we must collogue 75
sometimes, forswear sometimes.

MALEVOLE.

Be damn'd sometimes.

BILIOSO.

Right! "*Nemo omnibus horis sapit*": No man can be honest at all hours; necessity often depraves virtue.

MALEVOLE.

I will commend thee to the duke. 80

BILIOSO.

Do let us be friends, man.

MALEVOLE.

And knaves, man.

BILIOSO.

Right! Let us prosper and purchase; our lordships shall live, and our knavery be forgotten.

MALEVOLE.

He that by any ways gets riches, his means never shames 85
him.

BILIOSO.

True.

MALEVOLE.

For impudency and faithlessness are the main stays to greatness.

BILIOSO.

By the lord, thou art a profound lad. 90

MALEVOLE.

By the Lord, thou art a perfect knave. Out, ye ancient damnation!

BILIOSO.

Peace, peace! And thou wilt not be a friend to me as I am a knave, be not a knave to me as I am thy friend, and
disclose me. Peace! Cornets! 95

---

75. *collogue*] "to feign agreement or belief; to give a feigned assent" (*OED*, citing this as example).

78. *Nemo . . . sapit*] adapted from Pliny's *Naturalis Historia*, Bk. VII. xli. 2.

83. *purchase*] acquire wealth (illegally).

[V.iv]

Enter Prepasso and Ferrardo, two Pages with lights, Celso and Equato, Mendoza *in duke's robes, and Guerrino.*

MENDOZA.

On, on; leave us, leave us.

Exeunt all saving Malevole [*and* Mendoza].

Stay, where is the hermit?

MALEVOLE.

With Duke Pietro, with Duke Pietro.

MENDOZA.

Is he dead? Is he poisoned?

MALEVOLE.

Dead as the duke is. 5

MENDOZA.

Good, excellent. He will not blab; secureness lives in secrecy. Come hither, come hither.

MALEVOLE.

Thou hast a certain strong villainous scent about thee my nature cannot endure.

MENDOZA.

Scent, man? What returns Maria, what answer to our suit? 10

MALEVOLE.

Cold, frosty; she is obstinate.

MENDOZA.

Then she's but dead; 'tis resolute, she dies.
Black deed only through black deed safely flies.

MALEVOLE.

Pugh! "*Per scelera semper sceleribus tutum est iter.*" 15

MENDOZA.

What, art a scholar? Art a politician? Sure, thou art an arrant knave.

0.2. *and* Guerrino.] *Bilioso and Guerrino Q.*
1.1.] *after* Guerrino (*l. 0.2*) *Q.*
14. through black deed] *Q;* deedes *Q1–2.*
14. flies] *Q1–2;* fles *Q.*

10. *returns*] replies.
15. *Per . . . iter*] "The safe way to crimes is through crimes" (Seneca *Agamemnon* 115).

MALEVOLE.

Who, I? I have been twice an undersheriff, man. Well, I will go rail upon some great man, that I may purchase the bastinado, or else go marry some rich Genoan lady and 20 instantly go travel.

MENDOZA.

Travel when thou art married?

MALEVOLE.

Ay, 'tis your young lord's fashion to do so, though he was so lazy, being a bachelor, that he would never travel so far as the university; yet, when he married her, tails off, and 25 —catzo!—for England!

MENDOZA.

And why for England?

MALEVOLE.

Because there is no brothel houses there.

MENDOZA.

Nor courtesans?

MALEVOLE.

Neither; your whore went down with the stews, and your 30 punk came up with your Puritan.

MENDOZA.

Canst thou empoison? Canst thou empoison?

MALEVOLE.

Excellently; no Jew, 'pothecary, or politician better. Look ye, here's a box. Whom wouldst thou empoison?

18–31. Well . . . Puritan] *addition Q*, *preceded by:*

Enter Malevole and Mendoza.

Mendoza. Hast been with Maria?

Malevole. As your scrivener to your usurer, I have dealt about taking of this commodity; but she's cold-frosty.

18–31. *Well . . . Puritan*] see textual note, above; the extra passage seems to be an alternate reading for the first 18 lines that was improperly canceled and, as Collier suggests, "perhaps when it was wished to shorten the performance at all, the scene began here."

20. *bastinado*] cudgeling.

25. *tails off*] turns tail, takes to flight.

30–31. *your . . . Puritan*] Harrison cites Stow's *Survey of London*: "The Bordello or stews in Southwark, which had enjoyed peculiar privileges since the reign of Henry II, were put down by proclamation in 1546 . . . , about the same time as Puritanism was beginning."

30. *stews*] brothels.

31. *punk*] prostitute.

Here's a box [*giving it*] which, opened and the fume taken up in conduits thorough which the brain purges itself, doth instantly for twelve hours' space bind up all show of life in a deep senseless sleep. Here's another [*giving it*] which, being opened under the sleeper's nose, chokes all the power of life, kills him suddenly. 35–40

MENDOZA.

I'll try experiments; 'tis good not to be deceived. —So, so; catzo!

Seems to poison Malevole [, *who falls*].

Who would fear that may destroy?
Death hath no teeth or tongue;
And he that's great, to him are slaves 45
Shame, murder, fame, and wrong.—

Celso!

Enter Celso.

CELSO.

My honored lord?

MENDOZA.

The good Malevole, that plain-tongued man, alas, is dead on sudden, wondrous strangely! He held in our esteem good place. Celso, see him buried, see him buried. 50

CELSO.

I shall observe ye.

MENDOZA.

And, Celso, prithee, let it be thy care tonight
To have some pretty show, to solemnize
Our high installment—some music, masquery. 55
We'll give fair entertain unto Maria,
The duchess to the banish'd Altofront.
Thou shalt conduct her from the citadel
Unto the palace. Think on some masquery.

CELSO.

Of what shape, sweet lord? 60

35, 38. S.D.] *Dyce.*
35. taken] *Q;* tane *Q1–2.*
36. conduits] *Q* (*corrected*); comodites *Q* (*uncorrected*).
38. senseless] (sensles) *Q1–2;* cẽsles *Q.*
40. power] *Q, Q2;* pores *Q1.*
42.1. *who falls*] *Dyce.*
44. or] *Q;* nor *Q1–2.*
45. are] *Q, Q2;* one *Q1.*
47.1.] *after l. 40 Q; repeated again after* wrong (*l. 46*) *Q2; not in Q1.*

MENDOZA.

Why, shape? Why, any quick-done fiction,
As some brave spirits of the Genoan dukes
To come out of Elysium, forsooth,
Led in by Mercury, to gratulate
Our happy fortune; some such anything, 65
Some far-fet trick, good for ladies, some stale toy
Or other, no matter, so't be of our devising.
Do thou prepare't; 'tis but for a fashion sake.
Fear not; it shall be grac'd, man; it shall take.

CELSO.

All service. 70

MENDOZA.

All thanks; our hand shall not be close to thee; farewell.—
[*Aside.*] Now is my treachery secure, nor can we fall.
Mischief that prospers, men do virtue call.
I'll trust no man; he that by tricks gets wreaths
Keeps them with steel; no man securely breathes 75
Out of deserved ranks; the crowd will mutter, "Fool!"
Who cannot bear with spite, he cannot rule.
The chiefest secret for a man of state
Is to live senseless of a strengthless hate. [*Exit* Mendoza.]

MALEVOLE (*starts up and speaks*).

Death of the damn'd thief! I'll make one i' the masque; thou 80
shalt ha' some brave spirits of the antique dukes!

CELSO.

My lord, what strange delusion?

MALEVOLE.

Most happy, dear Celso, poison'd with an empty box!
I'll give thee all anon. My lady comes to court; there is a
whirl of fate comes tumbling on; the castle's captain 85
stands for me, the people pray for me, and the great Leader

65–67.] *Dyce; as prose Qq.*
68. for a fashion] *Q, Q2;* for fashion *Q1.*
75. with] *Q, Q1;* both *Q2.*
76. deserved] *Q, Q2;* distuned *Q1.*
79. S.D.] *Q1–2; not in Q.*

64. *gratulate*] salute.
66. *far-fet*] farfetched, i.e., cunningly devised.
71. *close*] closefisted, stingy.
74. *wreaths*] crowns (Harrison).
79. *senseless*] indifferent.

of the just stands for me. Then courage, Celso!
For no disastrous chance can ever move him
That leaveth nothing but a God above him. [*Exeunt.*]

[V.v]

Enter Prepasso *and* Bilioso, *two Pages before them;* Maquerelle, Biancha, *and* Emilia.

BILIOSO.

Make room there, room for the ladies! Why, gentlemen, will not ye suffer the ladies to be enter'd in the great chamber? Why, gallants! And you, sir, to drop your torch where the beauties must sit too.

PREPASSO.

And there's a great fellow plays the knave; why dost not strike him? 5

BILIOSO.

Let him play the knave, o' God's name; think'st thou I have no more wit than to strike a great fellow? —The music! More lights! Reveling-scaffolds! Do you hear? Let there be oaths enow ready at the door; swear out the 10 devil himself. Let's leave the ladies and go see if the lords be ready for them. *All save the* Ladies *depart.*

MAQUERELLE.

And, by my troth, beauties, why do you not put you into the fashion? This is a stale cut; you must come in fashion. Look ye, you must be all felt, felt and feather, a felt upon your 15 bare hair. Look ye, these tiring things are justly out of request now. And, do ye hear, you must wear falling bands, you must come into the falling fashion; there is such a deal o' pinning these ruffs, when the fine clean fall is worth all; and again, if you should chance to take a nap in 20 the afternoon, your falling band requires no poting stick to

89. S.D.] *Q1; not in Q, Q2.*
V.v] *no scene division in Qq.*
15–16. your bare hair] *Q, Q2;* your head *Q1.*

---

15. *felt*] i.e., a felt hat. 16. *tiring things*] headdresses.

17–18. *falling bands*] "a band or collar worn falling flat round the neck, in fashion during the seventeenth century" (*OED*).

21. *poting stick*] "a piece of stick, or iron, or bone, with which the plaits of ruffs were adjusted" (Dyce).

recover his form. Believe me, no fashion to the falling, I say.

BIANCHA.

And is not Signior St. Andrew a gallant fellow now?

MAQUERELLE.

By my maidenhead, la, honor and he agrees as well together as a satin suit and woolen stockings. 25

EMILIA.

But is not Marshall Make-room, my servant in reversion, a proper gentleman?

MAQUERELLE.

Yes, in reversion, as he had his office; as, in truth, he hath all things in reversion: he has his mistress in reversion, his clothes in reversion, his wit in reversion, and, indeed, is a 30 suitor to me for my dog in reversion. But, in good verity, la, he is as proper a gentleman in reversion as—and, indeed, as fine a man as may be, having a red beard and a pair of warp'd legs.

BIANCHA.

But, i'faith, I am most monstrously in love with Count 35 Quidlibet-in-Quodlibet. Is he not a pretty, dapper, unidle gallant?

MAQUERELLE.

He is even one of the most busy-fingered lords; he will put the beauties to the squeak most hideously.

[*Re-enter* Bilioso.]

BILIOSO.

Room! Make a lane there! The duke is ent'ring. Stand 40 handsomely, for beauty's sake; take up the ladies there! So, cornets, cornets!

22. falling] *Q*, *Q2;* falling band *Q1.*
23. St. Andrew] *Q*, *Q2; S. Andrew Iaques Q1.*
28. had] *Q*, *Q1;* did *Q2.*
34. warp'd] *Q1–2* (*warpt*)*;* wrapt *Q*.
36. unidle] *Q*, *Q2;* windle *Q1.*
39.1.] *Dyce.*

---

22. *to*] comparable to.

26. *in reversion*] "the right of succeeding to the possession of something after another is done with it, or simply of obtaining it at some future time" (*OED*).

33–34. *red . . . legs*] sometimes thought to be Marston laughing at himself.

[V.vi]

Enter Prepasso, *joins to* Bilioso; *two Pages and lights*, Ferrardo, Mendoza. *At the other door, two Pages with lights, and the Captain leading in* Maria. *The* Duke *meets* Maria *and closeth with her; the rest fall back.*

MENDOZA.

Madam, with gentle ear receive my suit;
A kingdom's safety should o'erpoise slight rites;
Marriage is merely nature's policy.
Then since, unless our royal beds be join'd,
Danger and civil tumult frights the state, 5
Be wise as you are fair, give way to fate.

MARIA.

What wouldst thou, thou affliction to our house?
Thou ever-devil, 'twas thou that banishedst
My truly noble lord.

MENDOZA.

I! 10

MARIA.

Ay, by thy plots, by thy black stratagems.
Twelve moons have suffer'd change since I beheld
The loved presence of my dearest lord.
O thou far worse than Death! He parts but soul
From a weak body; but thou soul from soul 15
Disseverest, that which God's own hand did knit;
Thou scant of honor, full of devilish wit!

MENDOZA.

We'll check your too intemperate lavishness.
I can and will!

MARIA.

What canst? 20

MENDOZA.

Go to; in banishment thy husband dies.

MARIA.

He ever is at home that's ever wise.

MENDOZA.

You'st never meet more; reason should love control.

---

2. *o'erpoise*] outweigh.
23. *You'st*] You must.

MARIA.

Not meet!

She that dear loves, her love's still in her soul. 25

MENDOZA.

You are but a woman, lady; you must yield.

MARIA.

O, save me, thou innated bashfulness,

Thou only ornament of woman's modesty!

MENDOZA.

Modesty! Death, I'll torment thee.

MARIA.

Do, urge all torments, all afflictions try; 30

I'll die my lord's as long as I can die.

MENDOZA.

Thou obstinate, thou shalt die. —Captain, that lady's life

Is forfeited to justice. We have examined her,

And we do find she hath empoisoned

The reverend hermit; therefore, we command 35

Severest custody. —Nay, if you'll do's no good,

You'st do's no harm. A tyrant's peace is blood.

MARIA.

O, thou art merciful! O gracious devil,

Rather by much let me condemned be

For seeming murder than be damn'd for thee! 40

I'll mourn no more; come, girt my brows with flowers;

Revel and dance, soul, now thy wish thou hast;

Die like a bride; poor heart, thou shalt die chaste.

Enter Aurelia *in mourning habit.*

AURELIA.

"Life is a frost of cold felicity,

And death the thaw of all our vanity." 45

Was't not an honest priest that wrote so?

MENDOZA.

Who let her in?

33. forfeited] *Q1–2;* forteified *Q.* 44.] *Q, Q2; Q1 assigns line to Maria.*

---

27. *innated*] innate.

44–45. *Life . . . vanity*] from an epigram in Thomas Bastard's *Chrestoleros* (1598), discovered by Bullen.

BILIOSO. Forbear!

PREPASSO. Forbear!

AURELIA.

Alas, calamity is everywhere.
Sad misery, despite your double doors,
Will enter even in court. 50

BILIOSO.

Peace!

AURELIA.

I ha' done. One word—take heed! I ha' done.

Enter Mercury *with loud music.*

MERCURY.

Cyllenian Mercury, the god of ghosts,
From gloomy shades that spread the lower coasts,
Calls four high-famed Genoan dukes to come 55
And make this presence their Elysium,
To pass away this high triumphal night
With song and dances, court's more soft delight.

AURELIA.

Are you god of ghosts? I have a suit depending in hell betwixt me and my conscience; I would fain have thee help 60 me to an advocate.

BILIOSO.

Mercury shall be your lawyer, lady.

AURELIA.

Nay, faith, Mercury has too good a face to be a right lawyer.

PREPASSO.

Peace, forbear! Mercury presents the masque. 65

Cornets: The song to the cornets, which playing, the masque enters; Malevole, Pietro, Ferneze, *and* Celso *in white robes, with duke's crowns upon laurel wreaths, pistolets and short swords under their robes.*

50.] *S.D.* "*Vnto Maria*" *follows in Q1.* 55. Genoan] *Q, Q2;* Genoa *Q1.*

---

53. *Cyllenian*] Mercury was born on Mount Cyllene.
54. *coasts*] regions, climes.
63. *right*] genuine.
65. *presents the masque*] "acts as presenter or introducer" (Harrison).

MENDOZA.
Celso, Celso, court Maria for our love.
—Lady, be gracious, yet grace.
Malevole *takes his* Wife *to dance.*

MARIA.
With me, sir?

MALEVOLE. Yes, more loved than my breath;
With you I'll dance.

MARIA. Why, then, you dance with death.
But, come, sir, I was ne'er more apt to mirth. 70
Death gives eternity a glorious breath;
O, to die honor'd, who would fear to die?

MALEVOLE.
They die in fear who live in villainy.

MENDOZA.
Yes, believe him, lady, and be rul'd by him.

PIETRO.
Madam, with me? Pietro *takes his wife* Aurelia *to dance.*

AURELIA. Wouldst then be miserable? 75

PIETRO.
I need not wish.

AURELIA.
O, yet forbear my hand! Away, fly, fly!
O, seek not her that only seeks to die!

PIETRO.
Poor loved soul!

AURELIA. What, wouldst court misery?

PIETRO.
Yes.

AURELIA. She'll come too soon. —O my griev'd heart! 80

PIETRO.
Lady, ha' done, ha' done.

66. court] *Q1–2;* count *Q.* 70. to] *Q;* for *Q1–2.*

---

70. *apt to*] given to.

Come, let's dance; be once from sorrow free.

AURELIA.

Art a sad man?

PIETRO.

Yes, sweet.

AURELIA.

Then we'll agree.

Ferneze *takes* Maquerelle; *and* Celso, Biancha; *then the cornets sound the measure, one change and rest.*

FERNEZE (*to* Biancha).

Believe it, lady: shall I swear? Let me enjoy you in private, and I'll marry you, by my soul. 85

BIANCHA.

I had rather you would swear by your body; I think that would prove the more regarded oath with you.

FERNEZE.

I'll swear by them both, to please you,

BIANCHA.

O, damn them not both to please me, for God's sake!

FERNEZE.

Faith, sweet creature, let me enjoy you tonight, and I'll 90 marry you tomorrow fortnight, by my troth, la.

MAQUERELLE.

On his troth, la! Believe him not; that kind of cony-catching is as stale as Sir Oliver Anchovy's perfum'd jerkin. Promise of matrimony by a young gallant, to bring a virgin lady into a fool's paradise, make her a great woman, and then cast 95 her off—'tis as common, as natural to a courtier, as jealousy to a citizen, gluttony to a Puritan, wisdom to an alderman, pride to a tailor, or an empty hand basket to one of these sixpenny damnations. Of his troth, la! Believe him not; traps to catch polecats! 100

82. Come,] *Q*, *Q2;* Come downe *Q1.*

98. hand basket] *not in Q1.*

92. *cony-catching*] knavery.

99. *sixpenny damnations*] "common whores of the streets" (Wood).

100. *polecats*] prostitutes.

MALEVOLE (*to* Maria).

Keep your face constant; let no sudden passion
Speak in your eyes. [*Reveals himself.*]

MARIA. O my Altofront!

PIETRO [*to* Aurelia]. A tyrant's jealousies
Are very nimble; you receive it all. [*Reveals himself.*]

AURELIA (Aurelia *to* Pietro).

My heart, though not my knees, doth humbly fall
Low as the earth, to thee. 105

PIETRO.

Peace! Next change; no words.

MARIA.

Speech to such, ay, O, what will affords!

Cornets sound the measure over again; which danced, they unmask.

MENDOZA.

Malevole! *They environ* Mendoza, *bending their pistols on him.*

MALEVOLE.

No!

MENDOZA.

Altofront! Duke Pietro! Ferneze! Ha! 110

ALL.

Duke Altofront! Duke Altofront! *Cornets, a flourish.*

MENDOZA.

Are we surpris'd? What strange delusions mock
Our senses? Do I dream? or have I dreamt
This two days' space? Where am I?

They seize upon Mendoza.

MALEVOLE.

Where an archvillain is. 115

MENDOZA.

O, lend me breath till I am fit to die!

102. S.D. *Reveals himself.*] *B-H-N.*
102. S.D. *to* Aurelia.] *marginal S.D. Q1; not in Q, Q2.*
103. S.D. *Reveals himself.*] *This edn.*
110. Pietro] *Q, Q2;* Lorenzo *Q1.*
116. breath till] *Q, Q2;* breath to liue till *Q1.*

---

108. S.D. *bending*] aiming.

For peace with heaven, for your own souls' sake,
Vouchsafe me life!

PIETRO.

Ignoble villain, whom neither heaven nor hell,
Goodness of God or man, could once make good! 120

MALEVOLE.

Base, treacherous wretch, what grace canst thou expect,
That hast grown impudent in gracelessness?

MENDOZA.

O, life!

MALEVOLE.

Slave, take thy life.
Wert thou defensed, through blood and wounds, 125
The sternest horror of a civil fight
Would I achieve thee; but, prostrate at my feet,
I scorn to hurt thee: 'Tis the heart of slaves
That deigns to triumph over peasants' graves;
For such thou art, since birth doth ne'er enroll 130
A man 'mong monarchs, but a glorious soul.
O, I have seen strange accidents of state!
The flatterer, like the ivy, clip the oak
And waste it to the heart; lust so confirm'd
That the black act of sin itself not sham'd 135
To be term'd courtship.
O, they that are as great as be their sins,
Let them remember that th' inconstant people
Love many princes merely for their faces
And outward shows; and they do covet more 140
To have a sight of these than of their virtues.
Yet thus much let the great ones still conceive:
When they observe not heaven's impos'd conditions,
They are no kings, but forfeit their commissions.

MAQUERELLE.

O good my lord, I have lived in the court this twenty year; 145

132–153.] *addition Q.*
139. princes] *Q (uncorrected)*; men *Q (corrected)*.
142. conceive] *Dyce;* conceale *Q.*
144. kings] *Q (uncorrected)*; men *Q (corrected)*.

125. *defensed*] provided with defenses, protected. 127. *achieve*] kill.
139, 144.] revision probably for politic reasons (Wood).

they that have been old courtiers and come to live in the city, they are spited at and thrust to the walls like apricocks, good my lord.

BILIOSO.

My lord, I did know your lordship in this disguise; you heard me ever say, if Altofront did return, I would stand for him. 150
Besides, 'twas your lordship's pleasure to call me wittol and cuckold; you must not think, but that I knew you, I would have put it up so patiently.

MALEVOLE. (*To* Pietro *and* Aurelia.)

You o'erjoyed spirits, wipe your long-wet eyes.
Hence with this man! (*Kicks out* Mendoza.) An eagle takes
not flies.— 155
(*To* Pietro *and* Aurelia.) You to your vows.— (*To* Maquer-
elle.) And thou unto the suburbs.—
(*To* Bilioso.) You to my worst friend I would hardly give:
Thou art a perfect old knave. —(*To* Celso *and the* Captain.)
All-pleased, live
You two unto my breast. —(*To* Maria.) Thou to my heart.
The rest of idle actors idly part; 160
And as for me, I here assume my right,
To which I hope all's pleas'd. To all, good night.

Cornets, a flourish. Exeunt omnes.

FINIS

154. S.P. MALEVOLE.] *not in Q.*
154. o'erjoyed] *Q, Q2;* are ioyd *Q1.*
160.] *Q, Q2; not in Q1.*

---

153. *put it up*] put up with it.
156. *suburbs*] brothels situated in the suburbs.

Epilogus

Your modest silence, full of heedy stillness,
Makes me thus speak: a voluntary illness
Is merely senseless; but unwilling error,
Such as proceeds from too rash youthful fervor,
May well be call'd a fault, but not a sin. 5
Rivers take names from founts where they begin.
Then let not too severe an eye peruse
The slighter brakes of our reformed Muse,
Who could herself herself of faults detect,
But that she knows 'tis easy to correct, 10
Though some men's labor. Troth, to err is fit,
As long as wisdom's not profess'd, but wit.
Then till another's happier Muse appears,
Till his Thalia feast your learned ears,
To whose desertful lamps pleas'd Fates impart 15
Art above Nature, Judgment above Art.
Receive this piece, which hope nor fear yet daunteth:
He that knows most, knows most how much he wanteth.

FINIS

---

1. *heedy*] heedful, attentive.
2. *illness*] flaw. 3. *merely*] utterly. 8. *brakes*] flaws.
11. *Though*] supply *'tis* after (B-H-N).
13. *another's*] Ben Jonson's? 14. *Thalia*] the comic Muse.
15. *desertful*] meritorious. 15. *lamps*] nocturnal studies (B-H-N).

Appendix

Chronology

Approximate years are indicated by *, occurrences in doubt by (?).

Political and Literary Events	*Life and Major Works of Marston*
1558	
Accession of Queen Elizabeth. Robert Greene born. Thomas Kyd born.	
1560	
George Chapman born.	
1561	
Francis Bacon born.	
1564	
Shakespeare born. Christopher Marlowe born.	
1570	
Thomas Heywood born.*	
1572	
Thomas Dekker born.* John Donne born. Massacre of St. Bartholomew's Day.	
1573	
Ben Jonson born.*	
1576	
The Theatre, the first permanent public theater in London, established by James Burbage.	John Marston born (probably at Coventry); christened at Wardington, October 7.
1577	
The Curtain theater opened. Holinshed's *Chronicles of England, Scotland and Ireland.*	

Drake begins circumnavigation of the earth; completed 1580.

1578

John Lyly's *Euphues: The Anatomy of Wit.*

1579

John Fletcher born.

Sir Thomas North's translation of Plutarch's *Lives.*

1580

Thomas Middleton born.

1583

Philip Massinger born.

1584

Francis Beaumont born.*

1586

Death of Sir Philip Sidney.

John Ford born.

1587

The Rose theater opened by Henslowe.

Marlowe's *TAMBURLAINE,* Part I.*

Execution of Mary, Queen of Scots.

Drake raids Cadiz.

1588

Defeat of the Spanish Armada.

Marlowe's *TAMBURLAINE,* Part II.*

1589

Greene's *FRIAR BACON AND FRIAR BUNGAY.**

Marlowe's *THE JEW OF MALTA.**

Kyd's *THE SPANISH TRAGEDY.**

1590

Spenser's *Faerie Queene* (Books I–III) published.

Sidney's *Arcadia* published.

Shakespeare's *HENRY VI,* Parts I–III,* *TITUS ANDRONICUS.**

1591

Shakespeare's *RICHARD III.**

1592

Marlowe's *DOCTOR FAUSTUS** and *EDWARD II.**

Shakespeare's *TAMING OF THE SHREW** and *THE COMEDY OF ERRORS.**

Death of Greene.

Matriculates at Brasenose College, Oxford, February 4.

Admitted to the Middle Temple, London, August 2.

1593

Shakespeare's *LOVE'S LABOUR'S LOST*;* *Venus and Adonis* published.

Death of Marlowe.

Theaters closed on account of plague.

1594

Shakespeare's *TWO GENTLEMEN OF VERONA*;* *The Rape of Lucrece* published.

Shakespeare's company becomes Lord Chamberlain's Men.

James Shirley born.*

Death of Kyd.

Receives B.A., March 23.

1595

The Swan theater built.

Sidney's *Defense of Poesy published.*

Shakespeare's *ROMEO AND JULIET,* A MIDSUMMER NIGHT'S DREAM,* RICHARD II.**

Raleigh's first expedition to Guiana.

1596

Spenser's *Faerie Queene* (Books IV–VI) published.

Shakespeare's *MERCHANT OF VENICE,* KING JOHN.**

1597

Bacon's *Essays* (first edition).

Shakespeare's *HENRY IV*, part I.*

1598

Demolition of The Theatre.

Shakespeare's *MUCH ADO*

The Metamorphosis of Pygmalion's Image and Certain Satires and *The*

*ABOUT NOTHING,** *HENRY IV*, Part II.*
Jonson's *EVERY MAN IN HIS HUMOR* (first version).
Seven books of Chapman's translation of Homer's *Iliad* published.

Scourge of Villainy, both published under pseudonym of "W. Kinsayder."

1599
The Globe theater opened.
Shakespeare's *AS YOU LIKE IT,** *HENRY V,** *JULIUS CAESAR.**
Dekker's *THE SHOEMAKERS' HOLIDAY.**
Death of Spenser.

The Scourge of Villainy, second edition with additional satire; included with *Pygmalion's Image* in Archbishop Whitgift's and Bishop Bancroft's "order of conflagration" of immoral books.
Henslowe records payment of £2 to "m^{r} maxton the new poete" for share in a now lost play (*LUST'S DOMINION*[?] or *ROBERT II, KING OF SCOTS*[?]), September 28. Revises *HISTRIOMASTIX* (?) for Children of Paul's.*

1600
Shakespeare's *TWELFTH NIGHT,** *HAMLET.**
The Fortune theater built by Alleyn.

*JACK DRUM'S ENTERTAINMENT,** *ANTONIO AND MELLIDA,** *ANTONIO'S REVENGE** (all for Children of Paul's).

1601
Shakespeare's *MERRY WIVES OF WINDSOR.**
Insurrection and execution of the Earl of Essex.

WHAT YOU WILL (Children of Paul's).*
Contributes to Robert Chester's *Love's Martyrs*, along with Jonson, Chapman, and Shakespeare.

1602
Shakespeare's *TROILUS AND CRESSIDA,** *ALL'S WELL THAT ENDS WELL.**

1603
Death of Queen Elizabeth; accession of James VI of Scotland as James I.
Florio's translation of Montaigne's *Essays* published.

Commendatory verses to Jonson's *SEJANUS.*
THE MALCONTENT (Children of Chapel Royal).*

Heywood's *A WOMAN KILLED WITH KINDNESS.* Shakespeare's company becomes the King's Men.	
1604 Shakespeare's *MEASURE FOR MEASURE,* OTHELLO.** Chapman's *BUSSY D'AMBOIS.**	Additions to *THE MALCONTENT* for the King's Men.* Acquires one-sixth interest in syndicate formed to manage newly formed Children of the Queen's Revels at Blackfriars—for whom all subsequent plays were written. *THE FAWN.**
1605 Shakespeare's *KING LEAR.** Bacon's *Advancement of Learning* published. The Gunpowder Plot.	*EASTWARD HO*, in collaboration with Chapman and Jonson. *THE DUTCH COURTESAN.** Married Mary Wilkes, daughter of rector of Barford St. Martin, in Wiltshire, with whom the couple may have resided until 1616.*
1606 Shakespeare's *MACBETH.** Jonson's *VOLPONE.** Tourneur's *REVENGER'S TRAGEDY.** The Red Bull theater built. Death of John Lyly.	*THE WONDER OF WOMEN; OR, THE TRAGEDY OF SOPHONISBA.** *City Pageant*, in honor of King James and his guest, King Christian of Denmark, July.
1607 Shakespeare's *ANTONY AND CLEOPATRA.** Beaumont's *KNIGHT OF THE BURNING PESTLE.** Settlement of Jamestown, Virginia.	An *Entertainment* for Alice, Dowager-Countess of Derby, at Ashby-de-la-Zouch, August.
1608 Shakespeare's *CORIOLANUS,* TIMON OF ATHENS,* PERICLES.** Chapman's *CONSPIRACY AND TRAGEDY OF CHARLES, DUKE OF BYRON.** Dekker's *Gull's Hornbook* published.	Imprisoned in Newgate, for unknown reasons, June 8. Sells share in Blackfriars to Robert Keysar, including probably unfinished play, *THE INSATIATE COUNTESS* (completed by 1613 by William Barksted).*

Richard Burbage leases Blackfriars Theatre for King's Company.
John Milton born.

1609

Shakespeare's *CYMBELINE*;* *Sonnets* published.
Jonson's *EPICOENE*.

Ordained deacon in parish church of Stanton Harcourt, Oxfordshire, September 24.
Ordained priest in same parish church, December 24.

1610

Jonson's *ALCHEMIST*.
Chapman's *REVENGE OF BUSSY D'AMBOIS*.*
Richard Crashaw born.

1611

Authorized (King James) Version of the Bible published.
Shakespeare's *THE WINTER'S TALE*,* *THE TEMPEST*.*
Beaumont and Fletcher's *A KING AND NO KING*.
Tourneur's *ATHEIST'S TRAGEDY*.*
Chapman's translation of *Iliad* completed.

1612

Webster's *THE WHITE DEVIL*.*

1613

The Globe theater burned.
Shakespeare's *HENRY VIII* (with Fletcher).
Webster's *THE DUCHESS OF MALFI*.*
Middleton's *A CHASTE MAID IN CHEAPSIDE*.
Sir Thomas Overbury murdered.

1614

The Globe theater rebuilt.
The Hope Theatre built.
Jonson's *BARTHOLOMEW FAIR*.

1616

Publication of Folio edition of Jonson's *WORKS*.

Priest at Christ Church, Hampshire, from October 10.

Death of Shakespeare.
Death of Beaumont.

1618
Outbreak of Thirty Years War.
Execution of Raleigh.

1620
Pilgrim Fathers land at Plymouth.

1621
Middleton's *WOMEN BEWARE WOMEN.**
Robert Burton's *Anatomy of Melancholy* published.
Andrew Marvell born.

1622
Middleton and Rowley's *THE CHANGELING.**
Henry Vaughan born.

1623
Publication of Folio edition of Shakespeare's *COMEDIES, HISTORIES, AND TRAGEDIES.*

1624

Only son John dies.

1625
Death of King James I; accession of Charles I.
Death of Fletcher.

1626
Death of Tourneur.
Death of Bacon.

1627
Death of Middleton.

1628
Ford's *THE LOVER'S MELANCHOLY.*
Petition of Right.
Buckingham assassinated.

1631
Shirley's *THE TRAITOR.*
Death of Donne.

Resigns living at Christ Church, September 16.

1632
Death of Dekker.*

1633

Donne's *Poems* published.
Massinger's *THE CITY MADAM*.*
Death of George Herbert.

William Sheares publishes unauthorized edition of six plays.

1634

Death of Chapman, Webster.*
THE TWO NOBLE KINSMEN published.

Marston dies in London "in Aldermanbury his house there," June 24; buried beside his father in Middle Temple Church.

1635

Sir Thomas Browne's *Religio Medici*.

1637

Death of Jonson.

1639

First Bishops' War.
Death of Carew.*

1640

Short Parliament.
Long Parliament impeaches Laud.
Death of Massinger, Burton.

1641

Irish rebel.
Death of Heywood.

1642

Charles I leaves London; Civil War breaks out.
Shirley's *COURT SECRET*.
All theaters closed by Act of Parliament.

1643

Parliament swears to the Solemn League and Covenant.

1645

Ordinance for New Model Army enacted.

1646

End of First Civil War.

1647

Army occupies London.
Charles I forms alliance with Scots.
Beaumont and Fletcher First Folio published.